Sanjeev Kapoor, host of the popular TV show 'Khana Khazana', now brings his priceless khazana of Indian recipes straight into your kitchen. In this book, the Master Chef has laid a feast of traditional and exotic Indian recipes.

Here is an assortment of delectable dishes that good food lovers and connoisseurs of Indian cuisine would relish. Whether it is a grand meal or an in-between snack that you want to surprise your guests with, this book offers an inspiring variety of tasty vegetarian dishes and irresistible desserts.

Each mouth-watering recipe which is the result of years of experience and careful experimentation, is presented in a manner that is easy to understand and prepare. You will find in this treasure of Indian cuisine, interesting new combinations of dishes and imaginative tips and ideas that add to the flavour.

Sanjeev Kapoor's innovations in cuisine have made him a household name in India and abroad. He has received widespread recognition and several awards for his mastery over the culinary art.

Sanjeev was an integral part of the catering team for the 1982 Asian Games and the SAARC summit at Shillong. He has organised food festivals in numerous countries and has also catered to VVIPs including the Prime Minister and the President of India. Sanjeev has launched a multimedia CD-ROM on Indian cooking and is currently working on an encyclopaedia of Indian cuisine. Get in touch with him on the website www.sanjeev kapoor.com.

This book helps you to master the art of cooking and express your love for your family and friends.

Happy Cooking

SANJEEV KAPOOR'S

KHAZANA OF INDIAN *Vegetarian* RECIPES

IN ASSOCIATION WITH ALYONA KAPOOR

POPULAR PRAKASHAN

POPULAR PRAKASHAN PVT. LTD.
35-C, Pt. Madan Mohan Malaviya Marg
Tardeo, Mumbai-400 034.

© 1999 by Sanjeev Kapoor

First Published 1999
First Reprint October 1999
Second Reprint July 2001
Third Reprint January 2002
Fourth Reprint October 2002

(3617)

ISBN - 81-7154-878-4

Design : Gopi Kukde *Photographs :* Satish Parab

PRINTED IN IN INDIA
By Alert Packaging House Pvt. Ltd., 326, A to Z Industrial Estate
Lower Parel, Mumbai and Published by Ramdas Bhatkal
for Popular Prakashan Pvt. Ltd.
35-C, Pt. Madan Mohan Malaviya Marg,
Tardeo, Mumbai-400 034.

FOREWORD

Cooking food is an art which comes naturally to some but there are others, like me, who have had to specially learn this delectable skill. Luckily, I have managed to understand the science behind this art which makes learning easier and quicker.

'Khana Khazana' on Zee TV has been a huge success and the innumerable letters received from loyal viewers of this programme prompted me to write this book on Indian food. This book is not merely a collection of recipes, but an attempt to encourage people to cook - and cook with confidence. Most of the recipes selected are very simple in the truest sense. They have been presented in a format that makes cooking systematic. Tips have been added in some cases to enable the reader to achieve better results and to encourage them to experiment while cooking.

While I would have loved to include in this book, every dish that one may desire to cook, obviously, space constraints meant that this was not possible. I have therefore tried to include as many of the standard and classic dishes as space would allow. Moreover, to keep the interest of the more adventurous cooks sizzlling, I have also included a number of interesting and unusual recipes. Having said so, the decision to put in or leave out a recipe has been a personal one and I must urge you to accept this arbitrary approach.

Ours has been a family of good food lovers. My father has always been the source of inspiration for all the creative work that I do with food today. His confident approach to food has inspired me from a very young age. I have always relished the unusual combinations that he keeps trying all the time. That is why, very candidly and rightly so, he says; *Beta tum to chef ho, hum to chef ke bhi baap hain*!

DEDICATION

This book is dedicated to
all the viewers of Khana Khazana
and my Family and Friends
who have been a constant support
to me at all times

ACKNOWLEDGEMENTS

Ajai Shah
Anil Bhandari
Anil Dharkar
Chef Harpal Singh Sokhi
Chef Inder Dev Boyal
Chef Rajeev Julka
Clea PR
Deepika & Vinod Sharma
Ganesh Pednekar
Gopi Kukde & his family
Hansal Mehta & Merlin Joseph
Hotel Vallerina, Khandala
J. M. Chaudhary
Jijesh Gangadharan
Khazana Restaurant, Dubai
Lalita & Hariharan
M. S. Gupta
Manoj Wagh
Mark Manuel
Meena & Ram Prabhoo
Mrs. & Mr. Kalyanpur
Neelima Acharya
Nina Murdeshwar
Rahee Dahake
Ramdas Bhatkal
Ramya Sarma
Rutika Samtani
S. K. Gupta
Sara & Vinod Nair
Satish Parab & his team
Sengupta B.
Subhash Chandra
Suresh Nair
Tanishq Consultants, New Delhi
Vijay Jindal
Vinayak Gawande
Zee Television

AUTHOR'S NOTE

All the recipes in this book have been written in a way that makes it easy to prepare even the more difficult dishes. The quantities are mentioned in teaspoons, tablespoons and cups so that the user is not scared of weights and measures mentioned in grams and litres. They have been first weighed and then converted into teaspoon/tablespoon/cup measures for the readers' benefit. These quantities have been arrived at after testing the recipes thoroughly.

All recipes serve four and the portion size of the serving takes into account the fact that the meal would be shared by a group of people. While cooking Indian food, the planned menu should have dishes from different sections, with varying colour, texture and taste.

A proper understanding of the ingredients used is vital to the art of cooking. A thumb rule to be followed is to take extra care while using certain ingredients such as salt, baking powder, red chilli powder. It may not matter much if you used two onions when the recipe required three. However, with ingredients like baking powder, any variation from the quantity stated may completely ruin the dish.

Normally, a recipe book mentions preparation time and total cooking time for each recipe. In this book we have done away with the practice deliberately as sometimes it can even become counter-productive. For instance, making a paste from ginger may take ten minutes, but these days you can even buy it off the shelf. However, actual cooking time needed has been mentioned at every stage of cooking.

A detailed glossary has been provided, at the end of the book not only on ingredients but also on some of the utensils commonly used in Indian cooking as also some of the processes. This should make life easier for the first time cooks.

PUBLISHER'S NOTE

The first edition of "Khazana of Indian Recipes" launched in January 1999 received an overwhelming response from readers all over the world and the book rapidly rose to the top of the bestseller list in India.

Sanjeev Kapoor received invitations from numerous cities to meet readers and have interactive sessions with them. In cooperation with leading booksellers all over the country we organised such sessions with readers in those cities. One message that came through was that some readers, who were strict vegetarians, were being offended by recipes and photographs of the non-vegetarian dishes.

A suggestion that was repeatedly made was to release a vegetarian edition of the book . This book is our attempt to respond to this suggestion. We would like to clarify that it is not a different book. The recipes in this book are all included in " Khazana of Indian recipes".

We have merely added a few new photographs of vegetarian recipes and deleted all the non-vegetarian recipes and photographs so as to be sensitive to vegetarian readers. We thank you for your suggestion and look forward to continuing feedback from you on our books.

Almonds	10-12	12 gms
Asafoetida (*hing*)	1/2 tspn	5 gms
Baking powder	1 tspn	3 gms
Black gram (*urad*), split	1 cup	220 gms
Black pepper powder	1 tspn	3 gms
Butter	1 tblspn	12 gms
Cashewnuts	10-12	7 gms
Cashewnuts paste	1 cup	140 gms
Chopped coriander leaves	1 cup	55 gms
Cloves	20	1 gms
Coriander (*dhania*) powder	1 tspn	2 gms
	1 tblspn	6 gms
Cumin (*jeera*) powder	1 tspn	2 gms
	1 tblspn	6 gms
Flour (*atta*)	1 cup	115 gms
Fresh cream	1 cup	250 mls
	1 tblspn	15 mls
Garam masala powder	1 tspn	2 gms
Garlic	6-8 cloves	5 gms
Garlic paste	1 tblspn	16 gms
Ghee	1 tblspn	7 gms
Ginger	1 inch	15-20 gms
Ginger paste	1 tblspn	16 gms
Gramflour (*besan*)	1 tblspn	10 gms
Grated cheese	1 cup	75 gms
Grated coconut	1 cup	175 gms
Green chillies	10	2 4 gms
	5	11 gms
Green coriander leaves	1 cup	35 gms
Green peas (frozen)	1 cup	110 gms
Honey	1 tblspn	20 gms
Lemon juice	(1/2 lemon) large sized 1 tspn	3 gms
Mawa (*khoya*)	1 cup	200 gms
Medium sized carrot	1	60 gms
Medium sized onion	1	90 gms
Medium sized potato	1	100 gms
Medium sized tomato	1	100 gms
Mustard (*rai*) powder	1 tspn	2 gms
Oil	1 tblspn	13 mls
Pigeon Pea, split (*tur dal*)	1 cup	225 gms
Red chilli (*mirch*) powder	1 tspn	2 gms
	1 tblspn	5 gms
Refined flour (*maida*)	1 tbslpn	8 gms
	1 cup	200 gms
Rice	1 cup	200 gms
Rice flour	1 tspn	3 gms
	1 tblspn	7 gms
	1 cup	115 gms
Salt	1 tspn	6 gms
Sugar	1 tblspn	14 gms
Tamarind pulp	1 tspn	6 gms
	1 tblspn	16 gms
Turmeric (*haldi*) powder	1 tspn	2 gms
	1 tblspn	7 gms
Vinegar	1 tblspn	11 gms
White pepper	55-60	3 gms
Yogurt	1 tblspn	15 gms

MEASUREMENTS

CONTENTS

VEGETABLES

ACCOMPANIMENTS

RICE AND ROTIS

SWEETS

BEETROOT SALAD WITH ORANGE DRESSING

INGREDIENTS

Beetroots	600 gms	White pepper powder	¼ tspn
Orange juice	¼ cup	Mustard powder	¼ tspn
Salad oil	1 tblspn	Orange rind	½ tspn
Salt	as per taste	Spring onion rings	¼ cup

METHOD OF PREPARATION

1. Boil the beetroots. When cool, peel and dice them into half-inch cubes. Chill them.
2. Mix orange juice, oil, salt, pepper, mustard powder and orange rind in a bowl and whisk till the mixture is homogeneous.
3. Pour the dressing over the beetroot pieces and garnish with rings of spring onion.

CARROT & CORIANDER SOUP

INGREDIENTS

Carrots ....650 gms	Bay leaves 2
Onion .... 1 medium sized	Peppercorn ....1 tspn
Garlic .... 6-8 cloves	Water ....1200 mls
Green coriander .... 1 packed cup	White pepper powder ....½ tspn
Butter .... 2 tblspns	Salt ....as per taste

METHOD OF PREPARATION

1. Wash, peel and roughly chop carrots. Peel and chop onion and garlic. Wash and finely chop fresh coriander leaves and reserve the stems.
2. Heat butter in a pan, add bay leaves, peppercorns, onions and garlic and fry for two minutes.
3. Add carrots, coriander stems and water and bring to a boil.
4. When the carrots are completely cooked, remove them and put in a blender to make a fine puree.
5. Reduce the stock slightly by boiling and strain.
6. Take the puree in a pan and add strained stock to reach the desired consistency. Bring to a boil again. Add white pepper powder dissolved in a little water. Add salt to taste. Stir in finely chopped fresh coriander leaves.
7. Serve piping hot.

INGREDIENTS

Green peas .... 500 gms
Onion ....1 medium sized
Ginger ....1 two inch piece
Garlic .... 8-10 cloves
Green chillies 2

Ghee or oil .... 3 tblspns
Cumin seeds .... ½ tspn
Bay leaves.................................2
Salt ....as per taste
Cream ....¼ cup

METHOD OF PREPARATION

1 Peel and boil the green peas. Blend in a blender to make a fine puree.

2 Peel and finely chop onion. Peel ginger and garlic and grind with green chillies to make a paste.

3 Heat ghee or oil in a pan; add cumin seeds and bayleaves, stir-fry for half a minute. Add chopped onion and sauté till onion turns light pink. Add ginger, garlic and green chilli paste. Sauté for a while.

4 Add green peas puree, cook for five minutes, stirring continuously. Add three cups of water and bring to a boil.

5 Season with salt and stir. Remove bay leaves and discard. Reduce heat and cook further for five minutes. This soup has a thick consistency, however you may make it of the consistency of your liking, by varying the quantity of water used.

6 Stir in fresh cream and serve hot, garnished with a swirl of cream.

3

MATAR KA SHORBA

INGREDIENTS

Fresh mushrooms ....200 gms
Onions .... 2 medium sized
Milk .... 300 mls
Bay leaves 2
Peppercorns 5-6
Cloves 4

Butter ....2 tblspns
Refined flour (*maida*) ....1 tblspn
Fresh cream .... ¾ cup
Salt ....as per taste
White pepper powder.......... ½ tspn
Nutmeg powder .... a pinch

METHOD OF PREPARATION

1   Clean and wash the mushrooms. Slice four to five pieces. Roughly chop the remaining mushrooms.

2   Roughly chop the onions.

3   Boil the milk along with bay leaves, peppercorns and cloves. Strain and keep the milk hot.

4   In a pan heat the butter. Add chopped onions and chopped mushrooms and cook till they are soft. Add the flour and sauté till there is no raw flavour coming from flour, taking care that the flour does not get burnt.

5   Pour the milk slowly and stir continuously to avoid lumps from forming.

6   Cook for five minutes. Puree the mixture when a little cold; do not puree it to a very thin consistency. The soup should have a smooth texture.

7   Bring it to a boil, correct the consistency by adding more milk if required. Add the cream (reserving a little for garnish), salt, pepper powder and nutmeg powder. Stir well.

8   Serve hot, garnished with mushroom slices and cream.

Chef's Tip : Use raw sliced mushrooms for garnishing. However, if you wish, you may sauté them in a little butter or oil and then use.

MUSHROOM SOUP

Beetroot salad with orange dressing

Carrot and Coriander soup, *Matar ka shorba*

RED PUMPKIN SOUP

INGREDIENTS

Onions ....2 medium sized	Salt ....as per taste
Red pumpkin (*lal bhopla*) ...600 gms	White pepper powder ....½ tspn
Butter ....2 tblspns	Lemon juice ....2 tspns
Bay leaves 2	Fresh cream ....¼ cup
Peppercorns 8-10	

METHOD OF PREPARATION

1. Peel and slice the onions. Peel and dice the red pumpkin. Heat butter in a pan, add bay leaves and peppercorns. Add onions and sauté for a while.
2. Add diced pumpkin, sauté for half a minute. Add sufficient water and cook until soft and fully done.
3. Strain excess water, reserve the stock and puree the vegetables.
4. Now add the stock to the puree to reach the correct consistency.
5. Add salt and pepper powder and bring to a boil. Add lemon juice.
6. Serve hot, garnished with cream.

Chef's Tip : This soup can be served in small sized red pumpkins. For that, ensure that the pumpkins that you buy are no bigger than the size of a coconut.

INGREDIENTS

Tomatoes ....4 large sized	Salt ....as per taste
Red gram, split *(toor dal)*...4 tspns	Coriander leaves.........for garnish
Whole red chillies 3	**For tempering**
Peppercorns 6	Oil...................................2 tblspns
Cumin seeds .... ¼ tspn	Mustard seeds ....½ tspn
Water ....5 cups	Asafoetida .... ¼ tspn
Ginger................. 1 one inch piece	Curry leaves 8-10

METHOD OF PREPARATION

1 Wash and chop tomatoes. Wash and chop coriander leaves. Pick, wash and boil dal with five cups of water. Strain the water and keep. Peel and roughly chop ginger.

2 Broil and grind together red chillies, peppercorns and cumin seeds with ginger.

3 Boil the dal water kept aside again with the chopped tomatoes, ground paste, and salt; cook until tomatoes are completely mashed.

4 Now heat the oil in a small pan. Add asafoetida, mustard seeds and curry leaves; when they crackle, add it to the above liquid. Mix and heat well once again for the flavours to mingle. Serve hot, garnished with chopped coriander leaves.

Chef's Tip : Chopped garlic added at the time of tempering gives this recipe a new dimension.

8

TOMATO RASAM

TOMATO SAAR

INGREDIENTS

Grated coconut .... 1 cup

Garlic .... 6 cloves

Cumin seeds .... 1 tspn

Green chillies 3-4

Coriander leaves .... ¼ cup

Ripe tomatoes ..... 5-6 large sized

Sugar .... 2-3 tblspns

Salt .... as per taste

Red chilli powder .... ½ tspn

Ghee.............................. 2 tblspns

Mustard seeds .... 1 tspn

Asafoetida .... a pinch

Curry leaves 8-10

METHOD OF PREPARATION

1 Make a paste of grated coconut, garlic cloves and cumin seeds. Slit green chillies into two. Chop the coriander leaves.

2 Wash, chop tomatoes roughly and add salt and red chilli powder. Transfer it to a pan and add three cups of water and bring it to a boil. Simmer for fifteen minutes and puree when it is a little cool.

3 Heat ghee in a pan and add mustard seeds, asafoetida and curry leaves. Add pureed tomatoes and slit green chillies and bring it to a boil and add sugar. Add coconut and spice paste.

4 Cook on a low heat for ten minutes. Correct seasoning.

5 Serve hot, garnished with chopped coriander leaves.

INGREDIENTS

Cauliflower .... 250 gms

Carrots .... 2 medium sized

Shelled green peas .... ¾ cup

Potatoes .... 2 medium sized

Green chillies 2

Yogurt .... 1 cup

Salt .... as per taste

Honey .... 2 tblspns

Rock salt powder .... ½ tspn

Fresh cream .... ¼ cup

Chopped coriander leaves......... 2 tblspns

METHOD OF PREPARATION

1 Clean and separate the cauliflower into small florets. Peel and dice the carrots into small pieces. Cook them in salted water. Refresh in cold water.

2 Boil green peas in salted water. Drain excess water. Refresh in cold water.

3 Boil, peel and dice the potatoes into small pieces. Cool them.

4 Wash green chillies and finely chop.

5 Whisk yogurt, salt, honey, rock salt powder and chopped green chillies with fresh cream.

6 Mix all the cooked vegetables with the yogurt dressing.

7 Chill and serve garnished with chopped coriander leaves.

VEGETABLE SALAD WITH YOGURT DRESSING

BATATA VADA

INGREDIENTS

Potatoes	600 gms	Salt	as per taste
Ginger	1 one inch piece	Soda bi-carbonate(baking soda)	a pinch
Garlic	10-12 cloves	Turmeric powder	¼ tspn
Green chillies	4-5	Chopped coriander leaves	2 tblspns
Gram flour (*besan*)	1 ½ cups	Oil	to fry
Red chilli powder	1 tspn		

METHOD OF PREPARATION

1. Boil, cool, peel and mash the potatoes and keep aside.
2. Make a paste of ginger, garlic and green chillies.
3. Prepare a thick batter of besan with water, red chilli powder, salt and soda bi-carbonate.
4. Heat a little oil. Add ginger-garlic-green chilli paste.
5. Add mashed potatoes and turmeric powder and mix well. Add chopped coriander leaves and salt to taste.
6. Let the mixture cool. When cold, form lemon sized balls.
7. Heat oil in a kadai. Dip the potato balls into the besan batter and deep fry in hot oil till light golden brown. Serve hot with chutney or sauce of your choice.

DHOKLA

INGREDIENTS

Rice .... 1 cup
Black gram skinless (*urad dal*) ..¼ cup
Yogurt ....¼ cup
Warm water .... 1 ½ cup
Salt ....as per taste
Ginger .... 1 one inch piece

Green chillies 4
Soda bi-carbonate (baking soda) .....½ tspn
Lemon juice ....1 tblspn
Oil ....2 tblspns
Coriander leaves .... 2 tblspns

METHOD OF PREPARATION

1 Dry roast the rice and the dal on medium heat for four to five minutes. Cool and grind into a semi-coarse powder.

2 Put the powder in a bowl. Add yogurt which should be a little sour and to this add warm water. Mix thoroughly so that no lumps are formed and the batter is of pouring consistency.

3 Add salt and let it ferment for eight to ten hours.

4 Make a paste of ginger and green chillies.

5 Once fermented, mix the ginger, green chilli paste with the batter.

6 Grease the dhokla platter or a thali. Boil water in the steamer/boiler.

7 Pour half of the batter in another vessel. In a small bowl, add one-fourth tspn soda bi-carbonate, half tspn oil and half tspn lemon juice. Add this to the batter and mix well. Repeat this for the remaining batter just before putting it in the steamer.

8 Pour this onto the greased platter and keep it in the steamer to steam for eight to ten minutes.

9 Check with a knife. If the knife comes out clean, it is cooked.

10 Sprinkle some finely chopped coriander leaves and serve hot with green chutney.

Chef's Tip : You can also put crushed peppercorn or red chilli powder over the dhokla. It is best enjoyed with ghee if desired.

12

INGREDIENTS

Gramflour (besan) .... 2 cups
Yogurt .... 1 cup
Chopped green chillies .... 1 tblspn
Chopped ginger .... 1 tblspn
Turmeric powder .... ½ tspn
Salt .... as per taste

Soda bi-carbonate (baking soda) .... 1 tspn
Oil .... 2 tblspns
Lemon 1
Mustard seeds .... 1 tspn
Chopped green coriander .... 2 tblspn
Grated fresh coconut .... ¼ cup

METHOD OF PREPARATION

1 Take gramflour in a bowl. Add beaten yogurt and warm water. Whisk nicely so that no lumps remain. The mixture should be of a slightly thick consistency. Add salt and leave it covered to ferment for three to four hours.

2 Grind green chillies and ginger into a paste.

3 When the gramflour and yogurt mixture has fermented, add ground chillies and ginger. Add turmeric powder and correct seasoning.

4 Keep the steamer ready on the flame.

5 Grease the dhokla mould/shallow cake tin or a thali with a little oil. In a small bowl take one teaspoon of soda bi-carbonate, one teaspoon oil and juice of a lemon. Mix and add to the gramflour mixture.

6 Pour the batter into the greased mould and steam for ten to twelve minutes. Proceed similarly with rest of the batter.

7 When a little cool, cut into squares and keep in a serving bowl/plate.

8 Heat oil in a small pan. Add mustard seeds. When the seeds begin to crackle remove and pour over the dhoklas.

9 Serve, garnished with chopped green coriander leaves and grated coconut.

KHAMAN DHOKLA

HARA BHARA KABAB

INGREDIENTS

Boiled potatoes...3-4 medium sized

Boiled green peas ....¾ cup

Spinach .... 100 gms

Chopped green chillies ....1 tblspn

Chopped green coriander..2 tblspns

Chopped ginger .... 1 tblspn

Chaat masala ....1 tspn

Salt ....as per taste

Cornflour (cornstarch) ...2 tblspns

Oil ....for deep frying

METHOD OF PREPARATION

1 Peel and grate boiled potatoes.

2 Mash boiled green peas.

3 Blanch spinach leaves in plenty of salted boiling water, refresh in cold water and squeeze out excess water. Finely chop.

4 Mix grated potatoes, peas and spinach. Add chopped green chillies, chopped green coriander, chopped ginger, chaat masala and salt. Add cornflour for binding.

5 Divide the mixture into twenty five equal portions. Shape each portion into a ball and then press it in between your palms to give it a flat tikki shape.

6 Heat oil in a kadai. Deep-fry the tikkis in hot oil for three to four minutes.

Chef's Tip : You may also shallow fry hara bhara kabab on a griddle plate or a tawa. It is recommended that you do not use colour in this recipe. If you feel you may increase the quantity of spinach leaves to give a dark green colour. In that case add a little more cornflour/cornstarch for binding.

Khandvi, Khaman dhokla, Patra

KHANDVI

INGREDIENTS

Gram flour (besan) .... 1 ¼ cups	Water .... ½ cups
Ginger ....1 one inch piece	Oil ....4 tblspns
Green chillies 2	Mustard seeds .... 1 tspn
Yogurt ....1 cup	Asafoetida ....a pinch
Salt ....as per taste	Grated coconut ....2 tblspns
Turmeric powder ....½ tspn	Chopped coriander leaves .. 2 tblspns
Lemon juice ....1 tblspn	

METHOD OF PREPARATION

1 Sieve the besan and keep in a bowl. Grind ginger and green chillies. Grease the reverse side of a few thalis or marble tabletop.

2 Make buttermilk with yogurt and water.

3 Mix the besan with ginger, green chillies, salt, turmeric powder, lemon juice and buttermilk. Take care that there are no lumps.

4 Cook this mixture over fire till it thickens into a thick batter. Stir constantly.

5 Quickly spread the mixture over the greased inverted thalis or marbled top as thinly as possible while the batter is still hot.

6 When cool, roll the layer towards you and cut into 1″ pieces.

7 Heat oil and add mustard seeds. When they splutter, add asafoetida and pour over the pieces.

8 Serve garnished with grated coconut and chopped coriander leaves.

Chef's Tip : Making Khandvi is an art, it takes some practise to get the correct consistency after cooking. Try small portions first.

INGREDIENTS

Black gram, skinless *(urad dal)* .... 1 cup

Salt .... as per taste

Asafoetida .... ¼ tspn

Curry leaves 8-10

Cumin powder .... 1 tspn

Crushed black peppercorns ....1 tspn

Oil ....to deep fry

METHOD OF PREPARATION

1 Wash and soak urad dal for six hours. Grind into a fine paste.

2 Add salt, asafoetida, curry leaves, cumin powder and crushed peppercorns to the batter and mix well.

3 Heat oil in a kadai.

4 Wet your palms and take batter into the palms. Shape into balls and make a hole with the thumb in the centre like a doughnut.

5 Deep-fry this in medium hot oil until golden brown and crisp.

6 Serve hot with sambhar and coconut chutney.

MEDU VADA

MIRCHI VADA

INGREDIENTS

Large green chillies 16

Boiled potatoes ....500 gms

Red chilli powder ....1 tblspn

Garam masala powder ....1 tblspn

Chaat masala ....1 tspn

Chopped green coriander ....1 tblspn

Salt ....as per taste

For batter

Gram flour *(besan)* .... 1 cup

Baking powder ....1 tspn

Red chilli powder ....1 tspn

Salt ....as per taste

Oil ....for deep-frying

METHOD OF PREPARATION

1 Slit green chillies and remove seeds.

2 Peel and grate boiled potatoes and add red chilli powder, garam masala powder, chaat masala, green coriander and salt. Mash and mix well. Divide this into sixteen equal portions.

3 Stuff a little of this mixture into the green chillies and also cover the chillies with this potato mixture.

4 Now prepare a thick batter using besan, baking powder, red chilli powder, salt and about one cup of water. Let the batter stand for ten minutes.

5 Heat oil in a kadai to a moderate temperature. Dip stuffed green chillies into the besan batter and deep fry until golden brown.

Chef's Tip : Select large sized green chillies for this recipe. It will not only give it a nice definite shape but also will not be very hot.

INGREDIENTS

Split green gram, skinless (*moong dal*)...1 cup
Cumin seeds ....1 tspn
Green chillies 2
Asafoetida ....a pinch
Salt ....as per taste
Cottage cheese (*paneer*) ....100 gms

Chopped onion.............................½ cup
Chopped tomato ....½ cup
Chopped coriander leaves ..... 2 tblspns
Red chilli powder ....½ tspn
Oil ....to shallow fry

METHOD OF PREPARATION

1 Pick, clean and wash moong dal. Soak moong dal in two cups of water for two hours. Grind soaked moong dal with cumin seeds and green chillies. Dissolve asafoetida in two tablespoons of water and mix it into the dal batter. Add salt and mix well.

2 Grate paneer and mix chopped onion, chopped tomato and chopped coriander leaves with this. Season with salt and red chilli powder. Keep aside.

3 Heat oil in a tawa or a frying pan. Spoon about one ¾ katori of batter onto the tawa and spread it to make a pancake with a diameter of about four to five inches. Shallow fry for about half a minute.

4 Sprinkle about two tablespoons of the paneer topping over the chillah. Spoon a little oil on the sides of the chillah and cook for fifteen seconds on medium heat.

5 Turn the chillah over and let it cook on the other side for two minutes on low to medium heat. Spoon oil on the sides of the chillah and turn it over. Cook for another minute on moderately high heat. Serve hot with mint chutney or chutney of your choice.

MOONG KE CHEELAY

PANEER KOLIWADA

INGREDIENTS

Cottage cheese *(paneer)*....300 gms

Gram flour *(besan)* ....½ cup

Cumin powder .... ½ tspn

Yogurt ....2 tblspns

Kashmiri red chilli powder.....2 tspn

Salt ....as per taste

Ginger paste .... 1 tblspn

Garlic paste ....1 tblspn

Lemon juice ....2 tblspns

Oil ....to fry

Chaat masala....................½ tspn

METHOD OF PREPARATION

1 Cut the paneer into finger size pieces (3" x ½" x ½").

2 Prepare a thick batter with besan, cumin powder, yogurt, red chilli powder, salt, ginger paste, garlic paste and lemon juice.

3 Marinate the paneer pieces in this batter for half an hour.

4 Heat oil in a kadai and deep fry the paneer pieces till crisp on the outside.

5 Serve hot, sprinkled with chaat masala.

Chef's Tip : To make Paneer koliwada extra crisp, add a tablespoon of cornstarch/ cornflour to the batter.

INGREDIENTS

Colocasia (*arbi*) leaves	12	Green chillies paste	1 tspn
Gram flour (*besan*)	1 ½ cups	Ginger paste	1 tspn
Turmeric	1 tspn	Oil	4 tblspns
Coriander powder	2 tspns	Jaggery	100 gms
Red chilli powder	1 tspn	Tamarind pulp	2 tblspns
Cumin powder	1 tspn	Mustard seeds	1 tspn
Sesame powder	2 tspns	Chopped coriander leaves	4 tblspns
Grated coconut	¼ cup	Asafoetida	¼ tspn
Salt	as per taste		

METHOD OF PREPARATION

1. Remove the thick stem from the leaves. Wash leaves and keep aside.
2. In a bowl take gram flour, turmeric powder coriander powder, cumin powder, red chilli powder, sesame powder, salt, green chillies' paste, ginger paste and two tblspns oil and mix well.
3. Mix the tamarind pulp and jaggery and add to the above mixture to make a paste.
4. Now spread the paste evenly on the back of each leaf, fold over the two sides and then roll.
5. Form into six inch rolls, making sure that all the batter is inside the leaf. Place the rolls on a sieve and steam.
6. Steam for about thirty to forty minutes or till cooked. Remove and let it cool. Cut into half centimetre thick pieces.
7. Heat oil in a kadai. Add mustard seeds. When they begin to crackle add asafoetida and then put in the steamed rolls. Sauté till golden brown.
8. Serve hot, garnished with grated coconut and coriander leaves.

PATRA

RICE PAKORAS

INGREDIENTS

Gram flour (besan) .... ½ cup

Cooked rice ....2 cups

Chopped green chillies ......1 tblspn

Chopped onion ....½ cup

Chopped green coriander ...1 tblspn

Chopped ginger ....1 tblspn

Chaat masala ....1 tspn

Salt ....as per taste

Oil .... for deep-frying

METHOD OF PREPARATION

1 Mix all the above ingredients except oil. Add one-fourth cup water to make a thick batter.

2 Heat oil in a kadai to a moderate heat.

3 Spoon the batter into hot oil by using a tablespoon and deep fry till light golden brown.

4 Drain on a paper napkin to remove excess oil and fry once again in very hot oil briefly.

5 Serve hot with chutney of your choice.

Chef's Tip : For this recipe you may also use leftover cooked rice.

VEGETABLE SAMOSA

INGREDIENTS

For dough

Flour (*maida*) ....:.... 1 cup
Carom seeds (*ajwain*) (optional)....½ tspn
Ghee/oil ....3 tblspns
Salt .... as per taste

For stuffing

Shelled green peas ....½ cup
Oil ....2 tblspns + for frying
Cumin seeds .... 1 tspn

Chopped ginger ....1 tspn
Chopped green chillies ....1 tspn
Potato cubes (½ cm) ....2 cups
Red chilli powder.......................1 tspn
Salt .... as per taste
Dry mango powder (*amchur*) .....1 tspn
Garam masala powder ....1 tspn
Chopped coriander leaves ....1 tblspn

METHOD OF PREPARATION

1 Mix the dough ingredients. Add water little by little and make a hard dough. Keep it under a wet cloth for ten to fifteen minutes.

2 Cook green peas in salted boiling water till soft. Refresh in cold water. Drain out excess water.

3 Heat oil in a pan, add cumin seeds and when they start to change colour, add chopped ginger, chopped green chillies and diced potatoes. Add red chilli powder, salt, amchur and garam masala powder. Stir well.

4 Sprinkle water and cook covered till potatoes are done. Add shelled green peas and mix well.

5 Divide the dough into sixteen equal portions and roll them into balls. Apply a little flour and roll them into four inch diameter elongated diskettes.

6 Cut into half, apply water on the edges. Shape into a cone and stuff it with the potato and peas filling. Seal the edges and deep fry in medium hot oil till crisp and golden brown.

7 Serve hot with tamarind chutney.

Mirchi vada, Samosa

Beans foogath

Dum ki arbi

INGREDIENTS

French beans .... 400 gms	Curry leaves 8-10
Onions .... one large sized	Salt ....as per taste
Green chillies 2	Grated coconut ....½ cup
Oil ....2 tblspns	Lemon 1
Mustard seeds .... 1 tspn	

METHOD OF PREPARATION

1 String and dice french beans finely. Peel onions and chop them. Wash green   chillies and chop them.

2 Heat oil in a kadai, add mustard seeds and curry leaves. When mustard seeds begin to crackle, add chopped onions and green chillies. Stir on a high flame for a minute. Do not brown onion.

3 Add diced french beans and salt. Cook covered on a low flame for five to seven minutes or till beans are cooked but are still a little crunchy.

4 Add grated fresh coconut and juice of a lemon. Mix well and serve hot.

Chef's Tip: Do not overcook beans as they tend to lose colour and also the texture. This dish can be also enjoyed cold. After cooling, or if some of it is leftover, keep the beans foogath in the refrigerator and while serving, garnish with chopped onions, chopped green coriander and a little lemon juice.

27

BEANS FOOGATH

SABUDANA VADA

INGREDIENTS

Sago *(sabudana)* ....1 ½ cups

Potatoes ....3 medium sized

Roasted peanuts ....1 cup

Green chillies 3

Chopped coriander leaves ...2 tblspns

Lemon juice ....1 tblspn

Salt ....as per taste

Oil ....to fry

METHOD OF PREPARATION

1. Soak the sabudana (in enough water to cover it) for about two hours. Drain out excess water. Boil, peel and mash the potatoes.

2. Coarsely grind the roasted peanuts. Finely chop the green chillies.

3. Mix together sabudana, mashed potatoes, ground peanuts, chopped green chillies and green coriander, lemon juice and salt. Mix thoroughly.

4. Form into sixteen lemon sized balls, flatten between your palms and deep fry in hot oil till golden brown.

5. Serve hot with chutney of your choice.

INGREDIENTS

Brinjal (*baingan*) ....1 kg	Cumin seeds .... 1 tspn
Onions .... 3 medium sized	Chopped ginger ....2 tspns
Tomatoes .... 4 large sized	Red chilli powder .... 2 tspns
Green chillies 2	Salt .... as per taste
Oil .... 3 tblspns	Chopped coriander leaves ......2 tblspns

METHOD OF PREPARATION

1. Prick brinjals and roast them over open flame or in a tandoor/pre-heated oven until skin starts peeling off and the brinjal starts to shrink. Let it cool. You can cool it by dipping it in water. Remove skin and mash it completely.

2. Peel onions and chop them. Wash tomatoes and chop them. Wash green chillies and chop them.

3. Heat oil in a kadai. Add cumin seeds. Cook for half a minute and add chopped onions and sauté until translucent. Then add chopped ginger, chopped green chillies and cook for half a minute.

4. Add red chilli powder and mashed roasted brinjals. Cook for seven to eight minutes over medium flame, stirring continuously. Add salt to taste.

5. Add chopped tomatoes and again cook on medium flame for seven to eight minutes till oil separates.

6. Garnish with chopped green coriander.

Chef's Tip: It is easy to remove skin of the roasted brinjal if it is dipped in water just after roasting. Use large sized round brinjals for this recipe. While buying, select brinjals that are light in weight in proportion to their size.

29

BAINGAN BHARTA

INGREDIENTS

Lady finger *(bhindi)* .... 500 gms
Onions .... 2 large sized
Green chillies 3-4
Oil .... 4 tblspns
Cumin seeds .... ½ tspn

Red chilli powder .... 1 tspn
Coriander powder .... 1 tblspn
Turmeric powder .... ½ tspn
Dry mango powder *(amchur)* .... 2 tspns
Salt .... as per taste

METHOD OF PREPARATION

1 Peel and slice the onions. Wash green chillies and slit them into two.

2 Wash and dry the bhindi or wipe bhindi with a wet cloth. Cut both the ends and make 2″ long pieces. Slit bhindi horizontally without cutting them into two.

3 Heat oil in a kadai and add cumin seeds. Add onions and sauté till light golden. Add green chillies and sauté for half a minute.

4 Add bhindi and sprinkle the red chilli, coriander and turmeric powders over the bhindi. Mix well. Cook covered over low fire stirring occasionally. Add salt and amchur. When bhindi is almost cooked, finish cooking by cooking it on high flame for two minutes.

Chef's Tip : You may use tiny onions for this recipe. Peel and make deep cross cuts in onions and stuff with a mixture of turmeric powder, coriander powder, red chilli powder, salt and amchur. Use same stuffing for bhindi and cook covered, with a little oil and green chillies.

BHINDI MASALA

CORN CAPSICUM MASALA

INGREDIENTS

Corn kernels .... 300 gms
Capsicums .... 3 medium sized
Onions .... 3 medium sized
Tomatoes .... 2 medium sized
Coriander leaves .... ¼ cup
Oil .... 3 tblspns
Cumin seeds .... ½ tspn
Ginger paste .... 2 tblspns
Garlic paste .... 1 tblspn

Red chilli powder .... 1 tspn
Coriander powder .... 1 tblspn
Cumin powder .... 1 tspn
Turmeric powder .... ½ tspn
Mawa (khoya) .... ½ cup
Garam masala powder .... 1 tspn
Salt .... as per taste
Fresh cream (optional) .... ¼ cup

METHOD OF PREPARATION

1. Boil corn in lots of water. Once cooked, drain out excess water and keep aside.

2. Wash, deseed and dice the capsicums into 1 cm sized cubes. Peel onions and chop them. Wash tomatoes and chop them finely. Wash and finely chop coriander leaves.

3. Heat oil in a kadai. Add cumin seeds, and when they begin to crackle, add chopped onions and sauté till golden brown.

4. Add ginger-garlic paste and cook for two to three minutes. Then add red chilli powder, coriander powder, cumin powder, and turmeric powder. Stir fry for a few seconds. Add chopped tomatoes and cook till oil leaves the masala, stirring continuously. Add mawa and half cup of water, mix well and cook for a minute.

5. Add diced capsicum and mix well. Finally add boiled corn, garam masala powder and salt. Mix and cook on low flame for four to five minutes.

6. Stir in fresh cream and chopped coriander leaves and serve hot.

Chef's Tip : This is a rich dish, to reduce calories go easy on mawa (khoya) and fresh cream. Use a little milk instead.

INGREDIENTS

Colocasia (*arbi*) ....700 gms	Green cardamom 4-6
Oil ....4 tblspns + for deep frying	Ginger paste .... 1 tblspn
Onions ....3 medium sized	Garlic paste ....1 tblspn
Poppy seeds (*khus khus*) ..... 3 tblspns	Coriander powder ....1 tspn
Yogurt ....2 cups	Grated nutmeg .... ¼ tspn
Red chilli powder ....½ tspn	Garam masala powder ....½ tspn
Turmeric powder ....½ tspn	Salt ....as per taste
Cumin powder .... 1 tspn	Fresh cream ....¼ cup

METHOD OF PREPARATION

1 Peel and cut arbi into one inch sized pieces. Deep fry arbi in hot oil till crisp and golden brown.

2 Peel onions and cut into halves. Add two cups of water and boil till soft. Drain out excess water, cool and grind to a smooth paste.

3 Dry roast poppy seeds and then soak in water for half an hour. Grind to a smooth paste.

4 Whisk the yogurt along with red chilli powder, cumin powder and turmeric powder.

5 Heat oil in a pan. Add green cardamom, when they start to change colour slightly, add boiled onion paste. Sauté till light golden brown. Add ginger paste, garlic paste and coriander powder. Mix well. Stir in poppy seeds paste and cook for a minute.

6 Add the whisked yogurt, bring it to a boil. Add fried arbi, grated nutmeg, garam masala powder and salt.

7 Cover the pan with a tight-fitting lid and simmer for thirty minutes. Alternatively cover the pan with aluminium foil or seal the lid with wheat flour dough, so that the aroma is contained in the pan and does not escape.

8 Just before serving, open the lid and stir in fresh cream.

DUM KI ARBI

GATTA CURRY

INGREDIENTS

For gattas

Gram flour (besan)	1 ½ cups
Yogurt	2 tblspns
Cumin	½ tspn
Red chilli powder	½ tspn
Chopped ginger	½ tspn
Chopped mint	1 tblspn
Turmeric powder	½ tspn
Salt	as per taste
Soda bi-carbonate (baking soda)	a pinch
Ghee/oil	to deep fry

For gravy

Onion	2 medium sized
Yogurt	1 ½ cups
Red chilli powder	1 tspn
Coriander powder	2 tspns
Turmeric powder	1 tspn
Ghee/oil	2 tblspns
Cumin seeds	1 tspn
Cloves	4
Asafoetida	a pinch
Salt	as per taste
Garam masala powder	½ tspn

METHOD OF PREPARATION

1. Mix all the gatta ingredients except ghee/oil. Add two tblspns water to make a hard dough. Divide into six equal portions, roll into cylindrical shaped gattas.
2. Cook in two cups of boiling hot water for ten to fifteen minutes. Drain and reserve the water for the gravy. Cut the gattas into 1 inch pieces.
3. Heat ghee/oil and deep fry the gattas until light golden brown.
4. Peel onions and grate them. Mix yogurt, red chilli powder, coriander powder and turmeric powder.
5. Heat ghee/oil in a pan, add cumin seeds, cloves and asafoetida. Cook until cumin seeds start to change colour. Add grated onion, cook on high heat for three minutes till light pink.
6. Add yogurt mixed with spices. Cook on a low flame for five minutes.
7. Add gattas and then the water in which gattas were boiled. Cook on low flame until gravy is thick. Correct seasoning by adding salt and garam masala powder. Serve hot.

INGREDIENTS

Cauliflower (small sized) 2	Cumin powder ....1 tspn
Salt ....as per taste	Red chilli powder .... 1 tblspn
Turmeric powder .... 1 tspn	Coriander powder .... 1 tblspn
Onions ....2 medium sized	Garam masala powder ....1 tspn
Melon seeds .... ½ cup + 1 tspn	Tomato puree ....½ cup
Oil ....3 tblspns	Mawa (*khoya*).........................½ cup
Ginger paste .... 1 tblspn	Fresh cream .... ½ cup
Garlic paste .... 1 tblspn	Chopped coriander leaves ....2 tblspns

METHOD OF PREPARATION

1 Remove stalks from cauliflower. Boil cauliflower in salted water with ½ tspn turmeric powder till half cooked. Peel onions and grate them. Soak ½ cup melon seeds in water for an hour and grind to a smooth paste.

2 Heat oil in a kadai. Add grated onions and sauté until golden brown in colour.

3 Add ginger paste, garlic paste, cumin powder, red chilli powder, coriander powder, remaining turmeric powder, garam masala powder and salt. Stir for half a minute.

4 Add tomato puree and cook till oil leaves the masala. Add melon seed paste dissolved in 1 cup of water. Bring to a boil. Add mawa. Mix well.

5 Add half-boiled cauliflower and cook covered on low heat or in a pre-heated oven for fifteen minutes. Top with fresh cream and simmer for five minutes.

6 Serve hot, garnished with chopped coriander leaves and melon seeds.

GOBHI MUSSALLAM

KADAI VEGETABLES

INGREDIENTS

French beans 10-12	Green chillies 3-4
Carrots ....2 medium sized	Ginger ....1 two inch piece
Capsicums ....2 medium sized	Coriander leaves ....¼ cup
Cauliflower ....¼ flower	Oil ....4 tblspns
Tomatoes ....3 large sized	Green peas ....¼ cup
Onions....................2 medium sized	Turmeric powder ....½ tspn
Coriander seeds ....1 tblspn	Coriander powder ....1 tblspn
Cumin seeds ....1 tspn	Red chilli powder ....1 tspn
Dried red chillies 4-5	Salt ....as per taste
Garlic ....12-15 cloves	Garam masala powder ....1 tspn

METHOD OF PREPARATION

1 String the beans and peel the carrots. Halve the capsicums and remove the seeds. Cut all the vegetables into ¼" cubes. Separate the cauliflower into small florets. Wash tomatoes and chop them roughly. Peel onions and slice them. Peel and wash ginger.

2 Grind coriander and cumin seeds and three red chillies coarsely.

3 Grind garlic, green chillies and half the ginger to a paste. Make julienne of the rest of the ginger. Finely chop the coriander leaves.

4 Heat oil in a pan. Add the coarsely ground masala. Add the sliced onions and sauté till golden brown.

5 Add ginger-garlic-green chilli paste and sauté for one minute. Add the vegetables except capsicum and stir. Cook covered on low heat till carrots are almost done. Sprinkle a little water if necessary.

6 Add turmeric powder, coriander powder and red chilli powder. Stir continuously. Add tomatoes, salt and half cup of water and cook till the vegetables are cooked and the water has dried up.

7 Add capsicum and salt, cook for four to five minutes on a low flame. Sprinkle garam masala powder.

8 Serve hot, garnished with ginger julienne and chopped coriander leaves.

KARELA MASALEDAAR

INGREDIENTS

Bitter gourd (*karela*) ...5-6 medium sized
Salt..................2 tblspns + as per taste
Oil ....3 tblspns + to fry
Onions ....2 medium sized

Turmeric powder ....1 tspn
Coriander powder .... 2 tspns
Dried mango powder (*amchur*)...1 tspn
Red chilli powder .... 1 tspn

METHOD OF PREPARATION

1 Peel and reserve the scrapings of the karelas. Give a slit on one side and remove all the seeds. Cut karelas into thin slices. Wash and rub two table spoons salt all over the karelas and its scrapings. Set aside for three to four hours. Wash thoroughly again and squeeze dry the karelas.

2 Heat oil in kadai. Deep fry the sliced karelas till dark brown and crisp. Remove the karelas and keep aside.

3 Slice onions. Heat oil in a kadai. Add sliced onions. Sauté for three to four minutes till they are translucent. Add scrapings of karela and let it cook till onions are a little brown. Add turmeric powder, coriander powder, dry mango powder and red chilli powder.

4 Add the fried karelas to the above mixture and cook covered on low flame for five to six minutes.

5 Add salt if needed. Serve hot with chappatis.

Chef's Tip : Rubbing salt on karela takes out the bitterness to a great extent, be generous with salt while applying on the karela slices and later wash them thoroughly.

INGREDIENTS

Potatoes .... 18-20 small sized
Oil .... for deep-frying
Dried kashmiri chillies 5-6
Yogurt ....2 cups
Cardamom powder .... ½ tspn
Dry ginger powder ....1 tspn
Fennel powder .... 2 tblspns

Mustard oil ....¼ cup
Clove powder .... a generous pinch
Asafoetida .... a pinch
Salt ....as per taste
Roasted cumin powder .... ½ tspn
Garam masala powder ....½ tspn

METHOD OF PREPARATION

1 Peel and prick the potatoes all over with the help of a fork. Keep in salted water for fifteen minutes. Heat oil in a kadai and fry the potatoes on medium flame till golden brown. Make a paste of dried Kashmiri red chillies.

2 Whisk the yogurt with Kashmiri red chilli paste, cardamom powder, dry ginger powder and fennel powder.

3 Heat mustard oil in a pan. Add clove powder and asafoetida. Add half a cup of water and salt and bring to a boil.

4 Stir in the yogurt mixture and bring it to a boil. Add fried potatoes and cook till the potatoes absorb the gravy and oil floats on top.

5 Serve hot, garnished with freshly roasted cumin powder and garam masala powder.

Chef's Tip: The process of pricking the potatoes makes them very light, if not, that means the pricking has not been proper or sufficient. Therefore it is a good idea to fry one potato and check. The size of the potato is also important, it should be of a small size but should not be very small.

Dum aloo served in most restaurants is very different from the recipe given here. However, I prefer this version.

KASHMIRI DUM ALOO

MALAI KOFTA CURRY

INGREDIENTS

For koftas
Potatoes .... 4-5 medium sized
Cottage cheese (*paneer*) .... 100 gms
Green chillies 2
Cornflour ....¼ cup
Salt ....as per taste
Raisins ....¼ cup
Oil ....for deep-frying
For gravy
Onions ....3 medium sized
Oil ....3 tblspns

Ginger paste ....1 tblspn
Garlic paste ....1 tblspn
Green chillies 2
Coriander powder ....1 tspn
Turmeric powder .... 1 tspn
Salt ....as per taste
Tomato puree ....½ cup
Red chilli powder ....1 tspn
Mawa (*khoya*).......................½ cup
Fresh cream ....½ cup
Garam masala powder .... 1 tspn

METHOD OF PREPARATION

1 Boil the potatoes, cool, peel and grate them. Grate paneer. Wash all green chillies, deseed and chop them fine. Peel onions, cut them into halves and boil with a cup of water for ten minutes. Drain excess water, cool onions and grind into a smooth paste.

2 Mix mashed potatoes, paneer, two chopped green chillies, cornflour and salt. Mix well. Divide into sixteen equal sized balls. Stuff raisins into them. Deep fry in hot oil until slightly coloured. Drain and keep aside.

3 Heat oil in a kadai. Add boiled onion paste and cook for five minutes. Add ginger paste, garlic paste, chopped green chillies, coriander powder, turmeric powder and salt.Cook for a minute. Add tomato puree and red chilli powder and cook on a medium flame for eight to ten minutes or till oil separates from the masala.

4 Mix mawa in two cups of water and add to the gravy. Bring it to a boil and simmer for ten minutes on a slow flame. Stir occasionally. Stir in fresh cream and garam masala powder.

5 Place warm koftas in a serving dish and pour hot gravy on top and serve.

Chef's Tip : Fry one kofta and check for binding, if it breaks, add a little more cornflour. Deep fry in hot oil.

INGREDIENTS

Shelled green peas .... 1 ½ cups
Mushrooms .... 200 gms
Oil .... 2 tblspns
Green cardamom 4
Cinnamon .... 1 one inch stick
Onions .... 2 large sized
Ginger paste .... 1 tblspn
Garlic paste .... 1 tblspn

Tomato puree .... ½ cup
Red chilli powder .... 1 tblspn
Coriander powder .... 1 tblspn
Turmeric powder .... 1 tspn
Garam masala powder .... 1 tspn
Salt .... as per taste
Cashewnut paste .... ½ cup

METHOD OF PREPARATION

1 Clean, wash and cut mushrooms in quarters. Peel onions and chop them finely.

2 Heat oil in a kadai. Add green cardamom, cinnamon stick and chopped onions and sauté until light golden brown.

3 Add ginger paste, garlic paste, and cook for half a minute. Add tomato puree, red chilli powder, coriander powder, turmeric powder, garam masala powder and salt and cook till oil leaves the masala.

4 Add cashewnut paste dissolved in one cup of water, stir well. Add a cup of water, bring it to a boil and then add green peas and mushrooms. Cook on high flame for seven to eight minutes or till green peas are fully cooked.

5 Cook on a low flame for five minutes. Serve hot.

MATAR MUSHROOM

METHI KELA BHAJI

INGREDIENTS

Fenugreek leaves (*methi*) ......3 cups

Ripe bananas 3-4

Ginger ....2 one inch pieces

Green chillies 3-4

Turmeric powder ....½ tspn

Coriander powder ....2 tsps

Cumin powder ....2 tspns

Oil ....4 tblspns

Mustard seeds ....½ tspn

Salt ....as per taste

METHOD OF PREPARATION

1. Separate the methi leaves from stems. Wash thoroughly under running water. Chop finely and keep aside.

2. Cut bananas into one inch thick roundels with their skin on. Peel ginger and wash green chillies. Make a paste of ginger and green chillies.

3. Heat oil in a kadai. Add mustard seeds. When they start to crackle, add the chopped methi leaves and salt. Cook for ten to fifteen minutes on medium heat. Add turmeric powder and mix. Add ginger-green chilli paste, stir fry for a minute. Add coriander and cumin powder. Mix well. Cook for one to two minutes.

4. Finally add the banana roundels. Correct seasoning. Cook covered on low heat for two minutes.

5. Serve hot with chappatis/rotis of your choice.

INGREDIENTS

Fenugreek leaves (*methi*) .... 2 cups
Shelled green peas .... 1 cup
Onions .... 2 medium sized
Ginger paste .... 1 tblspn
Garlic paste ....1 tblspn
Green chillies 3
Chopped coriander leaves .... 2 tblspns
Fresh corn kernels ....1 cup
Lemon juice ....1 tblspn

Yogurt ....½ cup
Turmeric powder .... a pinch
Red chilli powder .... 1 tspn
Oil ....2 tblspns
Cumin seeds ....1 tspn
Mawa (*khoya*) .... ½ cup
Salt ....as per taste
Fresh cream ....1 cup

METHOD OF PREPARATION

1 Peel onions and grate them. Wash green chillies and chop them fine. Set aside.

2 Clean the methi leaves, wash them thoroughly and chop. Add one tea spoon salt and set aside for half an hour. Squeeze dry and wash again.

3 Boil the corn in water with lemon juice till soft. Drain and keep aside. Wash the peas and boil in water. Drain and keep aside. Whisk the yogurt with turmeric and red chilli powders. Mash mawa and keep aside.

4 Heat oil in a pan. Add cumin seeds. When they start to change colour, add grated onions and cook till brown, stirring continuously. Add ginger and garlic pastes and continue to cook. Add chopped methi leaves and chopped green chillies. Cook till all the moisture dries up.

5 Add the yogurt mixture and cook till oil separates. Now add cooked corn and green peas. Add mashed mawa and one cup of water. Add salt to taste. Cook for ten minutes.

6 Stir in fresh cream and mix well. Simmer for five minutes. Serve hot with chopped coriander leaves.

METHI
MATAR
MAKAI

INGREDIENTS

Potatoes	2 medium sized	Cumin seeds	1 tspn
Broad beans (papdi)	12-15	Coriander seeds	1 tblspn
Shelled green peas	½ cup	Garlic cloves	8-10
Cauliflower	¼ flower	Turmeric powder	1 tspn
Carrots	2 medium sized	Salt	as per taste
Red pumpkin	100 gms	Groundnut oil	3 tblspns
Grated coconut	1 ½ cups	Mustard seeds	1 tspn
Tamarind pulp	2 tblspns	Split black gram (urad dal, dhuli)	1 tspn
Dried red chillies	4	Curry leaves	8-10

METHOD OF PREPARATION

1 Peel and dice the potatoes into 1" cubes. String the beans, halve them and cut them into one inch sized pieces. Wash cauliflower and separate the cauliflower florets. Peel and dice the carrots into 1" cubes. Peel and dice the pumpkin into 1" cubes.

2 Add warm water to one cup of grated coconut and extract thick and thin milk. Keep aside. Dissolve tamarind pulp in half cup of water.

3 Heat a little oil and sauté two dried red chillies, cumin seeds, coriander seeds, garlic and the remaining half cup of grated coconut till a nice aroma is given out. Grind into a fine paste with a little water.

4 Boil the vegetables in the thin coconut milk with turmeric powder, tamarind extract and salt till three-fourths done. Add the ground masala and cook for ten minutes.

5 Heat a little oil separately and add the remaining red chillies broken into two, mustard seeds and urad dal. Add curry leaves and add this to the vegetables.

6 Continue cooking the vegetables till done. Then add the thick coconut milk and simmer for two to three minutes. Serve hot with boiled rice.

Chef's Tip : If broad beans are not available replace them with french beans.

MIXED VEGETABLES IN COCONUT MILK

Mixed vegetables in coconut milk

Mirchi ka salan

Paneer jhalfraizee

INGREDIENTS

Dry red chillies 2	Oil ....3 tblspns
Onions ....2 medium sized	Cumin seeds ....1 tspn
Ginger .... 2 one inch pieces	Red chilli powder .... 1 ½ tspns
Green chillies 1-2	Turmeric powder ....1 tspn
Tomatoes ....2 medium sized	Vinegar .... 1 ½ tblspns
Capsicums ....2 medium sized	Salt .... as per taste
Cottage cheese (paneer) ....400 gms	Garam masala powder ....1 tspn
Coriander leaves ....¼ cup	

METHOD OF PREPARATION

1 Break the red chillies into two pieces.

2 Peel onions and cut into thick slices, separate the different layers of onion. Peel ginger and cut into julienne. Wash green chillies and chop them.

3 Cut the tomatoes and capsicums into half, remove the seeds and cut them into long slices with half centimetre width. Finely chop the coriander leaves. Cut the paneer into finger sized pieces.

4 Heat oil in a kadai. Add cumin seeds. When they start to change colour, add the halved red chillies. Add ginger julienne and sliced onions. Sauté for half a minute.

5 Add red chilli powder and turmeric powder. Stir well and then mix capsicum pieces and cook for two to three minutes. Add paneer fingers and toss. Add salt and vinegar and cook for two to three minutes. Stir in tomato pieces and garam masala powder.

6 Serve hot, garnished with chopped coriander leaves.

47

PANEER JHALFRAIZEE

INGREDIENTS

Green chillies (large) 18-20
Oil ....2 tblspns + to fry chillies
Sesame seeds .... 2 tblspns
Roasted peanuts .... ½ cup
Mustard seeds ....1 tspn
Coriander seeds ....1 tblspn
Cumin seeds ....1 tspn
Dry red chillies 2

Turmeric powder ....1 tspn
Onion ....1 medium sized
Ginger ....1 one inch piece
Garlic ....6-8 cloves
Curry leaves 8-10
Tamarind pulp ....2 tblspns
Salt .... as per taste

METHOD OF PREPARATION

1 Wash, wipe and slit green chillies lengthwise without cutting the chillies into two. Deep fry in hot oil for one minute. Remove on a paper towel and keep aside.

2 Peel and grate onion. Peel ginger and roughly chop. Dry roast sesame seeds, coriander seeds and cumin seeds. Make a paste of roasted sesame seeds, roasted peanuts, coriander seeds, cumin seeds, dry red chillies, ginger and garlic cloves.

3 Heat oil in a pan, add mustard seeds, let it crackle and add curry leaves. Now, add grated onion. Sauté until onion is light golden brown. Make sure to stir continuously.

4 Add turmeric powder and mix well. Add masala paste and cook for three minutes, stirring constantly. Stir in one and half cups of water and bring it to a boil. Reduce the heat and cook for ten minutes. Add tamarind pulp (dissolved in half a cup of water, if it is too thick).

5 Add fried green chillies and salt and cook on low heat for eight to ten minutes.

In Hyderabad, Mirchi ka salan is traditionally served as an accompaniment to biryanis. Some people like to add grated coconut to the masala paste, but I prefer Mirchi ka salan without coconut. This gravy is referred to as Tili (Til - Sesame) aur Falli (Moong falli - Peanuts) gravy.

48

INGREDIENTS

Spinach ....2 large bunches (900 gms)
Cottage cheese *(paneer)* .... 200 gms
Garlic ....8-10 cloves
Green chillies 2-3
Oil .... 3 tblspns

Cumin seeds ....½ tspn
Salt .... as per taste
Lemon juice ....1 tblspn
Fresh cream ....4 tblspns

METHOD OF PREPARATION

1 Remove stems and wash spinach thoroughly under running water. Blanch in salted boiling water for two minutes. Refresh in chilled water. Squeeze out excess water. Grind into a fine paste along with green chillies.

2 Dice the paneer into 1"x 1"x ½" pieces. Chop garlic and keep aside.

3 Heat oil in a pan. Add cumin seeds. When they begin to change colour, add chopped garlic and sauté for half a minute. Add the spinach puree and stir. Check seasoning. Add water if required.

4 When the gravy comes to a boil, add the paneer dices and mix well. Stir in lemon juice. Finally add fresh cream.

5 Serve hot.

Chef's Tip: Palak paneer tastes best without too many spices and herbs. To get best results, do not overcook spinach, as overcooking would not only adversely affect the bright green colour of spinach but also the taste.

PALAK PANEER

SHAAM SAVERA

INGREDIENTS

For kofta

Spinach	600 gms
Green chillies	3-4
Garlic	6-8 cloves
Cornflour (cornstarch)	3 tblspns
Salt	as per taste
Oil	to deep fry
Cottage cheese (paneer)	125 gms

For tomato gravy

Butter	3 tblspns
Whole garam masala	1 tblspn
Ginger paste	1 tblspn
Garlic paste	1 tblspn
Tomato puree	2 cups
Red chilli powder	1 tblspn
Garam masala powder	½ tspn
Sugar/honey	3 tblspns
Dried fenugreek leaves, crushed (kasoori methi)	½ tspn
Fresh cream	1 cup
Chopped coriander leaves	2 tblspns
Salt	as per taste

METHOD OF PREPARATION

1 Wash spinach under plenty of running water to get rid of any dirt. Blanch in boiling hot water and refresh in cold water. Squeeze out water and finely chop the spinach and also green chillies. Add half of chopped green chillies, salt, chopped garlic and cornflour to chopped spinach. Mix well and divide into twelve equal portions.

2 Grate paneer. Add salt and mash well. Divide into twelve equal balls.

3 Take spinach portions, flatten them on your palm and stuff paneer balls in them. Shape into balls. Deep fry in moderately hot oil for five minutes. Drain and keep aside.

4 Heat butter in a pan, add whole garam masala. When they crackle, add ginger-garlic paste and remaining chopped green chillies. Cook for two minutes.

5 Add tomato puree, red chilli powder, garam masala powder, salt and one cup of water. Bring it to a boil, reduce heat and simmer for ten minutes. Add sugar or honey and kasoori methi. Stir in fresh cream.

6 Serve koftas cut into halves on top of tomato gravy. Do not boil koftas in the gravy as they may break.

Chef's Tip : Before proceeding with all the koftas, deep fry one and check if they are breaking. If yes, add some more cornstarch in the spinach mixture and then deep fry in hot oil. Whole garam masala for this recipe consists of 4 green cardamon, 6 cloves and a bayleaf.

INGREDIENTS

Onions ....3 medium sized	Oil ....3 tblspns
Tomatoes .... 3 medium sized	Cumin seeds ....1 tspn
Ginger ....1 two inch piece	Milk ....3 cups
Green chillies 2	Red chilli powder .... 1 tspn
Soyabean granules ....200 gms	Turmeric powder ....½ tspn
Coriander leaves ....¼ cup	Salt ....as per taste

METHOD OF PREPARATION

1   Peel and finely chop the onions. Peel ginger, wash green chillies and make a paste of ginger and green chillies. Thoroughly wash coriander leaves and finely chop them. Wash and chop tomatoes.

2   Wash soyabean granules with lukewarm water. Drain and then soak in warm milk for half an hour.

3   Heat oil in a pan. Add cumin seeds. When they start to change colour, add chopped onions and fry till light golden brown. Add ginger, green chilli paste and cook for half a minute.

4   Add chopped tomatoes and cook for four to five minutes. Add red chilli powder and turmeric powder. Cook till oil leaves the masala.

5   Add the soyabean granules and mix well. Cook covered till soya granules are cooked. This normally takes about ten minutes. Add a little water if required. Add salt and cook till it is almost dry.

6   Serve hot, garnished with chopped coriander leaves.

51

SOYABEAN GRANULES SABZI

INGREDIENTS

Small sized potatoes 6-8
Yam *(kand)* .... 100 gms
Raw bananas 2
Small brinjals 3-4
Broad beans *(papdi)* 25-30
Garlic .... 6-8 cloves
Green chillies 4
Ginger .... 2 one inch pieces
Coriander leaves .... 1 cup
Oil .... 5 tblspns
Asafoetida .... a pinch

Mustard seeds .... 1 tspn
Salt .... as per taste
Turmeric powder .... 1 tspn
For muthiya
Gram flour *(besan)* .... ¼ cup
Salt .... as per taste
Fenugreek leaves .... ½ cup
Ginger .... 1 half inch piece
Green chillies 1-2
Oil .... to deep fry

METHOD OF PREPARATION

1 Wash, peel and dice potatoes, yam and raw bananas. Wash and chop coriander leaves.

2 Wash brinjals and slit them into four without cutting the stem.

3 Make a paste of garlic, green chilli and ginger. Mix chopped coriander to the paste.

4 Mix all the muthiya ingredients except oil and prepare a stiff dough by using a little water. Divide into small portions and shape each into one inch long, half inch thick rolls. Deep fry in hot oil, till golden brown. Drain and keep aside.

5 String beans and cut into one inch long pieces.

6 Heat oil in a thick bottomed handi, add asafoetida and mustard seeds. When mustard seeds crackle, add ground masala and broad beans. Mix well. Place the rest of the vegetables in layers one on top of the other (interspread with masala and broad beans). Sprinkle salt and turmeric powder. Cook for five minutes on high flame.

7 Pour one cup of water, cover and simmer on a very low flame for ten to fifteen minutes.

8 Add fried muthiyas and again simmer for fifteen minutes. Shake the vegetables occasionally but do not use a spoon to stir.

9 Serve hot, garnished with grated coconut.

Chef's Tip : Traditionally Undhiyo is served with a lot of oil floating on top. You may vary the quantity of oil used as per your taste. Use surati papdi, (a special variety of broad beans) and purple kand (yam) for this recipe for best results.

UNDHIYO

BEETROOT RAITA

INGREDIENTS

Beetroots .... 2 medium sized

Yogurt .... 3 cups

Roasted cumin powder ....1 tspn

Red chilli powder ....1 tspn

Salt .... as per taste

METHOD OF PREPARATION

1 Boil beetroot. Peel, cool and dice into half centimeter sized pieces. Keep aside.

2 Beat yogurt to a smooth consistency. You can also strain the yogurt through a muslin cloth to get a smooth consistency.

3 Mix chopped beetroots with yogurt. Add roasted cumin powder, red chilli powder and salt.

4 Mix well and serve chilled.

Chef's Tip : The bright and dark colour of beetroot will bleed and change the colour of the yogurt to dark pink. Plan the rest of your meal accordingly.

INGREDIENTS

White gram, split *(urad dal)*....2 cups

Cumin seeds ....1 tspn

Fennel seeds *(saunf)* .... ½ tspn

Cashewnuts 15-20

Raisins ....2 tblspns

Black pepper corns .... ½ tspn

Salt .... as per taste

Oil ....to fry

Yogurt .... 6 cups

Roasted cumin powder .... 1 tspn

Red chilli powder ....1 tspn

Chopped coriander leaves ..... for garnish

Ginger julienne .... for garnish

Tamarind chutney ... as accompaniment

METHOD OF PREPARATION

1   Soak urad dal in enough water for six hours. Grind to a paste; the batter should be thick, not runny. Add cumin seeds, saunf and salt and mix well. Chop cashewnuts and raisins. Mix well.

2   Heat oil in a kadai. Pour a small ladle full of dal batter on a plastic sheet of 6"x 6". Spread the batter into a circle of 2 ½ diametre. Place a teaspoon of cashewnut and raisin stuffing in the center. Hold two top corners of the plastic sheet and bring towards you to join them with the other two corners. This will fold the batter into crescent shape. Gently slide the gujia into hot oil.

3   Deep fry the gujias till golden brown. Soak in warm water.

4   Beat yogurt to a smooth consistency, add salt.

5   Squeeze the gujias and put in the yogurt.

6   Sprinkle roasted cumin powder, red chilli powder, chopped coriander leaves and ginger julienne before serving.

7   Serve topped with tamarind chutney.

Chef's Tip : I have seen my mother use milk poly-bags instead of plastic sheets. The thickness of these bags is just right for this purpose. However cut open the bag and wash before use.

54

DAHI
GUJIA

Palak wali dal, Sookhi moong dal, Dal pakhtooni

INGREDIENTS

Black gram, whole *(urad)* ...... 1 cup

Salt .... as per taste

Ginger paste .... 2 tblspns

Garlic paste .... 2 tblspns

Red chilli powder ....1 tblspn

Butter .... 100 gms

Fresh Cream ....1 cup

Tomato puree .... 1 ½ cups

Garam masala powder ....2 tspns

METHOD OF PREPARATION

1 Pick and wash whole black urad. Soak it in four cups of water for eight to ten hours or overnight.

2 Cook it in four to five cups of water along with salt, red chilli powder and ginger paste. Bring it to a boil. Reduce flame and simmer for about an hour or till it is completely cooked and tender.

3 Melt butter in a thick bottomed pan and add garlic paste dissolved in half a cup of water. Cook for two minutes, stirring constantly.

4 Add tomato puree, butter and garam masala powder, add cooked dal to this and cook on a low flame for an hour. Stir occasionally. Add water if required.

5 Add fresh cream, correct seasoning and simmer for another ten minutes. The consistency of this dal is quite thick.

6 Serve hot with bread of your choice.

Chef Kapoor enjoys it with Pudina parantha!

DAL PAKHTOONI

DAHI VADA

INGREDIENTS

White gram, split *(urad dal)* .... 1 cup
Cumin seeds .... 1 tspn
Salt ....as per taste
Asafoetida .... a pinch
Oil ....for deep frying

Yogurt .... 3 cups
Roasted cumin powder ....1 tspn
Red chilli powder ....1 tspn
Chopped green coriander ....1 tblspn

METHOD OF PREPARATION

1 Pick, wash and soak dal in two cups of water for six to eight hours.

2 Drain and grind into a fine and fluffy paste. Add cumin seeds, salt and asafoetida and then whisk the mixture to incorporate air into it.

3 Heat oil in a kadai to moderate heat. Take about two tblspns of dal mixture on your wet palm and make a hole in the centre with your thumb, shape like a doughnut and lower into the hot oil. Deep fry the vadas till golden brown.

4 Drain and soak in warm water.

5 Beat yogurt with a whisk to make it smooth. Add salt and mix well.

6 Squeeze the vadas to remove excess water and add into the yogurt. Let them soak for at least fifteen to twenty minutes before serving.

7 Garnish with roasted cumin powder, red chilli powder and chopped coriander. Serve cold.

Chef's Tip : You may top it with tamarind chutney.

INGREDIENTS

Bottlegourd *(lauki/doodhi)* .....250 gms	Cumin seeds ....1 tspn
Salt .... as per taste	Red chilli powder .... ½ tspn
Yogurt, chilled...................... 3 cups	

METHOD OF PREPARATION

1 Peel, wash and grate lauki. Boil grated lauki with a little salt for five minutes. Drain out water and cool grated lauki.

2 Whisk chilled yogurt and mix salt and red chilli powder. Add cooked lauki and mix well.

3 Dry roast cumin seeds and make a coarse powder. Serve lauki raita topped with cumin powder.

Chef's Tip : Ensure to squeeze out excess water from cooked lauki.

LAUKI RAITA

MASALEDAAR CHHOLAY

INGREDIENTS

Chick peas *(kabuli chana)*........ 1 ½ cups	Tomatoes ....4 medium sized
Salt .... as per taste	Coriander leaves ....¼ cup
Tea leaves ....2 tspns	Oil .... 4 tblspns
Dried Indian gooseberry *(amla)*..... 3-4	Cumin seeds ....2 tblspns
Onions .... 3 large sized	Coriander powder ....3 tspns
Ginger ....2 one inch pieces	Red chilli powder ....1 tspn
Garlic ....8-10 cloves	Pomegranate seeds *(anardana)*
Green chillies 2	powder (coarse) ....1 tblspn

60

METHOD OF PREPARATION:

1 Soak the chana overnight in water. Boil in the same water with salt, dried amla and tea leaves (tied in a piece of muslin cloth) till tender. Remove amla and tea leaves.

2 Peel and chop the onions. Peel ginger and garlic. Wash green chillies and make a paste of ginger, garlic and green chillies. Wash and chop the tomatoes and coriander leaves. Dry roast cumin seeds, cool and grind to a powder.

3 Heat oil in a pan, add chopped onions and sauté till brown. Add ginger-garlic-green chilli paste and sauté for sometime.

4 Add coriander powder, ground roasted cumin seeds, red chilli, turmeric and anardana powders and cook till oil separates.

5 Add drained chana and mix well. Add tomatoes and a little cooking liquor and salt if required. Cook till the chanas are well mixed with the gravy.

6 Serve hot, garnished with coriander leaves.

Chef's Tip : If you like, you may add boiled and diced potatoes.

INGREDIENTS

Split green gram *(moong dal, dhuli)*...¾ cup	Cumin seeds .... 1 tspn
Salt .... as per taste	Onions .... 2 medium sized
Turmeric powder .... 1 tspn	Green chillies 2
Spinach .... 15-20 leaves	Ginger .... 1 one inch piece
Oil .... 2 tblspns	Garlic .... 6-8 cloves
Asafoetida .... a pinch	Lemon juice .... 1 tspn

METHOD OF PREPARATION

1 Pick, wash and boil moong dal with salt and turmeric powder in five cups of water. Cook till dal is fully cooked.

2 Wash spinach leaves thoroughly under cold running water. Then roughly shred them. Peel onions and chop them finely. Wash green chillies, deseed and chop them finely. Peel and chop garlic, keep aside. Wash and chop ginger.

3 Heat oil in a kadai. Add asafoetida and cumin seeds. When cumin seeds start to change colour, add chopped onions and chopped green chillies. Cook till onions are soft and translucent.

4 Add chopped ginger and garlic, cook for half a minute.

5 Add the boiled dal. Bring to a boil and add shredded spinach and lemon juice.

6 Simmer for two minutes and serve hot.

PALAK WALI DAL

RAJASTHANI PANCHMEL DAL

INGREDIENTS

Split gram *(chana dal)* ....¼ cup
Whole green gram *(moong)*.........¼ cup
Split black gram, skinless *(urad dal)*.....¼ cup
Pigeon peas, split *(toor dal)*.........¼ cup
Red lentils *(masoor)* ....¼ cup
Salt ....as per taste
Ginger ....1 one inch piece
Dried red chillies................................2
Coriander powder ....1 tspn
Green chillies 2

Coriander leaves ....2 tblspns
Cumin powder ....1 tspn
Red chilli powder ....½ tspn
Turmeric powder ....½ tspn
Tomatoes ....2 medium sized
Oil ....3 tblspns
Cumin seeds ....½ tspn
Cloves 4-5
Asafoetida .... a pinch
Garam masala powder ....½ tspn

METHOD OF PREPARATION

1   Soak the pulses for at least two hours. Then boil them in salted water with turmeric powder till done. Wash green chillies, coriander leaves and peel ginger.

2   Make a paste of ginger and green chillies. Chop the coriander leaves. Wash and chop the tomatoes.

3   Heat oil in a pan. Add asafoetida, cumin seeds, cloves and dried red chillies. When cumin starts to change colour, add ginger-green chilli paste and sauté for sometime.

4   Add cumin powder, coriander powder and red chilli powder. Add the tomatoes and cook till oil separates. Add cooked lentils and water if required.

5   Cook for ten minutes, stirring well. Add garam masala powder and serve hot.

INGREDIENTS

Red kidney beans *(rajma)* ..... 1 ½ cups	Coriander powder .... 1 tblspn
Oil ....3 tblspns	Turmeric powder ....½ tspn
Bay leaves 2	Cumin powder .... 1 tspn
Onions ....2 medium sized	Tomatoes .... 3 medium sized
Ginger .... 1 one inch piece	Garam masala powder .... 1 tspn
Garlic .... 6-8 cloves	Chopped fresh coriander ....1 tblspn
Red chilli powder ....2 tspns	Salt .... as per taste

METHOD OF PREPARATION

1   Soak rajma overnight in five cups of water.

2   Boil rajma or pressure cook till fully cooked and soft. Wash and peel ginger. Chop it finely. Chop garlic. Wash and chop tomatoes and peel and chop onions.

3   Heat oil, add bay leaves, chopped onions and sauté till onions are golden brown in colour. Add chopped ginger and garlic and cook for a minute.

4   Add red chilli powder, coriander powder, turmeric powder, cumin powder and stir. Add chopped tomatoes and cook till tomatoes are cooked and oil leaves the masala.

5   Add boiled rajma along with its cooking liquor and cook on a low flame for fifteen minutes, stirring in between. Add garam masala powder and cook for five minutes. Garnish with chopped fresh coriander. Serve hot with steamed rice.

In my mother's house, Mothi (Rajma) - Chawal has always been a Sunday lunch treat, week after week, month after month, year after year....!

63

RAJMA RASMISA

SOOKHI MOONG DAL

INGREDIENTS

Split green gram skinless
(moong dal, dhuli) .... 1 ¼ cups
Salt .... as per taste
Ginger .... 2 one inch pieces
Green chilli 1
Chopped coriander leaves .... 1 tblspn

Oil .... 3 tblspns
Cumin seeds .... ½ tspn
Asafoetida .... a pinch
Red chilli powder .... 1 tspn
Turmeric powder .... ½ tspn
Lemon juice .... 2 tspns

METHOD OF PREPARATION

1   Wash and soak the moong dal in water for half an hour. Boil dal with salt and turmeric powder till it is just cooked but not mashed.

2   Drain excess water, if any.

3   Peel ginger and wash green chilli. Chop ginger and green chilli.

4   Heat oil in a kadai. Add cumin seeds and asafoetida. Once the cumin seeds start to change colour, add chopped ginger and green chilli and sauté for half a minute.

5   Add red chilli powder and cooked dal. Mix and season with lemon juice and salt if required. Mix lightly, taking care not to mash the cooked dal and cook till dry.

6   Serve hot, garnished with chopped coriander leaves.

INGREDIENTS

Refined flour *(maida)* .... 2 ½ cups
Yogurt ....½ cup
Baking powder ....½ tspn
Soda bi-carbonate (baking soda) .... a pinch

Salt ....1 tspn
Sugar ....2 tspns
Oil ....2 tblspns + for frying

METHOD OF PREPARATION

1   Take flour and add baking powder, soda bi-carbonate and salt. Mix well and pass it through a sieve.
2   Mix yogurt and sugar. Add this to the flour and add about a cup of water and mix gradually to make a soft dough by light kneading.
3   Incorporate two tblspns oil into the dough and cover the dough with a wet cloth. Keep it aside for an hour.
4   Divide it into sixteen equal portions, roll them into balls. Cover and keep to ferment for ten minutes.
5   Grease your palms with a little oil and flatten the balls. Roll into five inch diameter diskettes.
6   Heat oil in a kadai and deep fry bhaturas on high flame till light brown on both sides.

Chef's Tip: You can make bhaturas of oval shape by pulling the rolled diskettes from opposite sides.

65

BHATURA

INGREDIENTS

Whole wheat flour *(atta)* ..... 1 ¼ cups	Steamed rice ....1 cup
Salt ....1 tspn	Red chilli powder ....½ tspn
Yogurt .... ¼ cup	Cumin powder ....½ tspn
Ghee ....2 tblspns	Green chillies 2
Onion ....1 medium sized	Oil ....to cook parantha

METHOD OF PREPARATION

1 Sieve whole wheat flour along with salt. Make a soft dough with yogurt, two tablespoons ghee and half cup of water. Cover with a moist cloth and set aside for half an hour.

2 Knead again and divide into four equal parts. Make balls and press between palms of your hand to make pedhas.

3 Peel and chop onion finely. Wash and chop green chillies.

4 Mix cooked rice with red chilli powder, cumin powder, chopped green chillies, chopped onions and salt.

5 Roll out each pedha into 3″ diameter disc.

6 Stuff rice mixture in the flattened pedha and shape into a pedha again.

7 Roll out into a 7″ diameter disc using a rolling pin.

8 Heat a tawa. Place the parantha over it. Turn over once and spread some oil around it. Turn over again and spread a little more oil on the other side. Cook till both sides are well cooked.

9 Serve hot with fresh yogurt and pickle of your choice.

Chef's Tip : You can use leftover rice for this recipe and the rice need not be reheated. It can be used straight out of the refrigerator.

CHAWAL KA PARANTHA

KHASTA KACHORI

INGREDIENTS

Refined flour .... 2 cups	Asafoetida .... a pinch
Salt .... as per taste	Coriander powder .... 1 tspn
Soda bi-carbonate (baking soda) ..... ¼ tspn	Cumin powder .... ¼ tspn
Oil .... 2 tblspns + to fry	Red chilli powder .... ½ tspn
Water .... ½ cup	Fennel powder .... ¼ tspn
Ginger .... 1 one inch piece	Sugar .... ½ tspn
Green Chillies 2-3	Salt .... as per taste
Split black gram (*urad dal*) .... ¹/₃ cup	Ghee .... 4 tblspns

METHOD OF PREPARATION

1 Sieve the flour, salt and soda bi-carbonate together. Add two tblspns of ghee and rub between your palms to get bread crumb texture.

2 Knead into a soft dough with water. Cover with a moist cloth and set aside.

3 Finely chop ginger and green chillies.

4 Soak the urad dal for an hour. Then coarsely grind using a little water.

5 Heat oil in a kadai. Add chopped ginger, chopped green chillies, asafoetida and all the powdered masalas. Stir well and add ground dal. Cook till all the moisture is almost dried up.

6 Add sugar and salt and mix well. Remove off the flame. Let the mixture cool.

7 Make twelve balls of the flour dough. Flatten each ball between your palms so that they are thinner around the edges and thicker in the centre.

8 Place a little stuffing in the centre and bring the edges together to form a ball. Flatten slightly.

9 Heat oil in a kadai. Fry kachoris on a slow flame till golden brown and crisp.

10 Serve with tamarind chutney.

INGREDIENTS

Rice .... 1 ½ cups	Fenugreek seeds *(methi seeds)* ...½ tspn
Salt .... as per taste	Peanuts .... ½ cup
Oil/ghee ....2 tblspns	Mustard seeds (optional) .... ½ tspn
Asafoetida .... a pinch	Curry leaves 10-12
Dried red chillies 2	Lemon juice .... 3 tblspns
Split black gram *(urad dal)* ..... 1 tblspn	Turmeric powder ....½ tspn
Split gram *(chana dal)* ....1 tblspn	Grated fresh coconut(optional) ..1 tblspn

METHOD OF PREPARATION

1 Pick, wash and soak rice for about thirty minutes. Drain and then boil in plenty of boiling salted water until almost done. Drain and keep aside.

2 Heat oil/ghee in a shallow pan or a kadai. Add a pinch of asafoetida. Add dried red chillies broken into two, urad dal, chana dal and methi seeds. Cook until dals change colour to light brown.

3 Add peanuts and mustard seeds. Let mustard seeds crackle, then add curry leaves. Mix turmeric powder in this. Stir fry for half a minute. Add cooked rice, salt and lemon juice.

4 Garnish with grated coconut.

Chef's Tip: You can use roasted or fried peanuts for this recipe.

LEMON RICE

LUCHI

INGREDIENTS

Refined flour *(maida)* .... 2 cups   Water .... 1 cup approximately
Salt .... 1 tspn   Oil .... for deep frying
Ghee .... 1 tblspn

METHOD OF PREPARATION

1. Sieve flour with salt. Add ghee and make a soft dough with water. Keep covered with a moist cloth for half an hour.
2. Divide into twenty equal parts and make small balls.
3. Roll into 3″ diameter discs.
4. Heat oil in a kadai and fry the luchis till well puffed and cream coloured.
5. Serve hot with dal or any curry of your choice.

INGREDIENTS

Ginger ....2 one inch pieces	Coriander leaves ....2 tblspns
Green chillies 4-5	Ghee .... 3 tblspns
Turmeric powder .... ½ tspn	Cumin seeds ....1 tspn
Corn kernels ....1 cup	Asafoetida ....a pinch
Lemon juice ....2 tblspns	Salt .... as per taste
Rice .... 1 ¼ cups	Water for cooking rice ......3 ½ cups

METHOD OF PREPARATION

1 Peel and chop ginger finely. Wash and chop green chillies and keep aside. Wash and chop the fresh coriander leaves. Wash and soak the rice for half an hour.

2 Boil the corn in water with lemon juice till tender. Drain and keep aside.

3 Heat ghee in a degchi. Add cumin seeds. Once they start to change colour, add asafoetida and then add chopped ginger, chopped green chillies and turmeric powder. Mix well and cook for two or three minutes.

4 Add cooked corn and water and bring to a boil. Add rice and salt, mix and cook on a slow flame till rice is cooked and the khichdi is of the right consistency.

5 Garnish with chopped coriander leaves and serve hot with yogurt, papad and pickle of your choice.

Chef's Tip : Consistency of khichdi is a matter of personal preference. If you want khichdi to be not-too-runny, add a little less water.

MAKAI KI KHICHDI

METHI PARANTHA

INGREDIENTS

Wheat flour (atta) .... 1 cup	Oil .... 4 tblspns
Red chilli powder .... 1 tspn	Chopped fenugreek (methi) leaves .... 1 cup
Salt .... to taste	Ripe banana .... half
Yogurt .... ½ cup	Gram flour (besan) .... ½ cup
Ghee .... 3 tblspns	

METHOD OF PREPARATION

1 Sieve atta, besan along with salt and red chilli powder. Peel and mash banana.
2 Add chopped methi leaves, ghee and yogurt and mix well. Add mashed banana, two tblspns of oil and knead into a stiff dough. Keep covered with a damp cloth and leave it for twenty minutes.
3 Divide into eight equal portions. Roll out each into a 5″ diskette.
4 Cook on a hot tawa, applying a little oil till both sides are cooked and lightly golden brown.

Chef's Tip : This dough does not need any water and the parantha can stay fresh for three or four days. It is ideal food on long journies.

NAAN

INGREDIENTS

Refined Wheat Flour *(maida)*	...... 4 cups	Salt	1 tspn
Milk	1 cup	Onion seeds	2 tspns
Baking powder	1 tspn	Egg	1
Water	as required	Sugar	2 tspns
Soda bi-carbonate (baking soda)	½ tspn	Butter	2 tspns
Oil	2 tblspns	Yogurt	2 tblspns

METHOD OF PREPARATION

1. Sieve flour with baking powder, baking soda and salt. Add sugar, egg, milk, yogurt and water. Knead well into a medium soft dough.
2. Apply a little oil and keep it under wet cloth for one hour.
3. Make eight equal portions of the dough. Apply a little oil and put the onion seeds on top.
4. Press sides first and then centre of the dough ball. Give a round flat shape. Pick in hand and pat to give it a round shape of about six inches diameter.
5. Stretch it from one side to give a triangular shape. Put it on a cloth and put it on a pre-heated tandoor wall or cook in a pre-heated oven (200 degrees Celsius).
6. Remove using skewers when it is crisp and brown on both sides.
7. Serve hot, topped with butter.

Chef's Tip : If you don't consume eggs, proceed with this recipe without egg. The loss of taste and texture would hardly be noticeable.

INGREDIENTS

Spinach leaves *(palak)* .... 500 gms
Green chillies 3-4
Whole wheat flour *(atta)* .... 1 ¼ cups

Salt .... as per taste
Ghee .... ½ cup

METHOD OF PREPARATION

1 Clean and wash the palak leaves. Set aside 100 gms and chop them coarsely. Blanch the rest and refresh in cold water.

2 Wash and remove the seeds and roughly chop the green chillies.

3 Puree the blanched palak leaves and green chillies together.

4 Sieve the atta with salt and make a soft dough with palak puree, chopped palak and water if needed. Cover with a moist cloth and keep aside for thirty minutes.

5 Divide into eight equal portions. Roll out each, spread some ghee and fold into half.

6 Fold again into a quarter. Roll out into triangles with each side of 6" approximately.

7 Heat a tawa and place the parantha over it. Turn it and spread some ghee round it. Turn again and spread some ghee on the other side too. Cook till both sides are evenly cooked.

8 Serve hot with yogurt.

73

PALAK
PARANTHA

INGREDIENTS

Whole wheat flour *(atta)* ..... 2 cups

Mint leaves *(pudina)* ....1 cup

Salt ....1 tspn

Butter ....3 tblspns

METHOD OF PREPARATION

1. Sieve whole wheat flour and salt together. Add water to whole wheat flour and salt mixture and knead into a stiff dough. Keep it covered with a wet cloth for twenty to twenty-five minutes.
2. Dry half the mint leaves on a hot tawa, cool and crush to a powder. Chop the remaining mint leaves.
3. Mix the rest of the mint leaves with the dough.
4. Divide the dough into six equal portions. Shape them into balls.
5. Now roll the dough to a medium chappati and smear with butter and sprinkle with flour. Fold the chappati like a fan and twist it back into the form of a ball. Keep aside for five minutes.
6. Roll out each portion into a parantha of 5"-7" diametre and cook on a hot tawa applying a little oil till both sides are lightly golden brown.
7. Sprinkle the dried pudina leaves on the parantha and crush between your palms.

Chef's Tip : If you are cooking Pudina parantha in the tandoor apply a little water on the side that you are going to stick on the tandoor wall.

PUDINA PARANTHA

PUDINA PULAO

INGREDIENTS

Basmati rice .... 1 ¾ cups	Green cardamom 4-6
Ginger ....2 one inch pieces	Cloves 4-6
Yogurt ....¾ cup	Large cardamom 3-4
Mint leaves (pudina)..........1 ½ cups	Black pepper corns 8-10
Ghee .... 3 tblpsns	Salt ....as per taste
Bay leaves 2	Water for cooking ....3 ¼ cups

METHOD OF PREPARATION

1 Wash and soak the rice in water for half an hour.

2 Peel ginger and grind it into a paste. Whisk yogurt and keep aside.

3 Pluck the pudina leaves. Wash nicely. Reserve a few for garnish and chop the rest.

4 Heat ghee in a thick-bottomed pan. Add bay leaves, green cardamom, large cardamom, cloves and black peppercorns. When they start to crackle, add ginger paste. Mix well and stir in yogurt, and cook for two to three minutes.

5 Add water and bring to a boil. Add salt.

6 Drain and add rice. Bring to a boil. Add chopped mint leaves, mix lightly. Cover the pan and cook on a slow heat for about eight to ten minutes or till rice is completely cooked.

7 Serve hot, garnished with mint leaves.

INGREDIENTS

Basmati rice .... 1 ½ cups
Onions .... 2 medium sized
Tomatoes 3-4
Cauliflower cut into florets ....¾ cup
Carrots .... 2 small sized
French beans 10-12
Shelled green peas .... ½ cup
Salt .... as per taste

Ghee .... 3 tblspns
Cumin seeds .... 1 tspn
Green cardamom 3-4
Large cardamom 3-4
Cinnamon .... 1 one inch stick
Cloves 4-6
Water .... 3 cups

METHOD OF PREPARATION

1 Wash and soak the rice in water for an hour.
2 Peel and slice onions. Wash and chop tomatoes and keep aside.
3 Peel carrots and dice them into half inch cubes. String beans and cut them into half inch sized pieces.
4 Heat ghee in a thick-bottomed pan, add cumin seeds, green cardamom, large cardamom, cinnamon and cloves. Once they start to crackle, add sliced onions and cook till onions become translucent.
5 Add chopped tomatoes and cook till oil can be seen on the sides of the pan. Add three cups of water and bring to a boil. Add carrots and cook for five minutes.
6 Drain excess water from rice and add rice to the pan. Once it starts to boil, add green peas, cauliflower florets, diced beans and salt. Reduce the heat and cover the pan. Cook till rice is completely done.
7 When the rice is cooked, open the pulao, and lightly stir with a spatula so as to ensure that no lumps are formed.

SABZI AUR TAMATAR KA PULAO

TAMARIND RICE

INGREDIENTS

Rice .... 1 ¼ cups	Tamarind pulp .... 3 tblspns
Whole red chillies 6	Asafoetida .... ¼ tspn
Mustard seeds .... 1 tspn	Split gram *(chana dal)* ......2 tblspns
Roasted peanuts .... ¼ cup	Sesame seeds (optional) .....3 tblspns
Curry leaves 10-12	Split black gram
Oil .... 3 tblspns	*(urad dal, dhuli)* ....2 tblspns
Ginger .... 1 one inch piece	Turmeric .... ½ tspn

METHOD OF PREPARATION

1 Wash and soak the rice in water for half an hour.
2 Drain and cook rice in plenty of boiling water. Once the rice is cooked, strain and spread on a plate. Sprinkle a little oil and mix lightly.
3 Keep aside two red chillies for roasting. Chop ginger finely.
4 Heat two tblspns oil and add four dried red chillies, mustard seeds, chana dal, and urad dal. Sauté for two to three minutes till dals have a brown colour. Add turmeric powder, asafoetida, curry leaves, roasted peanuts and chopped ginger. Stir, fry for half a minute.
5 Add tamarind pulp and salt to the above mixture and cook for some time.
6 Dry roast sesame seeds and grind coarsely with two red chillies.
7 Mix in the dry mixture and tamarind mixture to the rice. Mix well and serve.

BASOONDI

INGREDIENTS

Almonds .... ½ cup	Milk .... 1 ½ lts
Charoli seeds (*chironji*) ...... 2 tblspns	Sugar .... ¾ cup
Pistachio nuts 8-10	Saffron .... a pinch

METHOD OF PREPARATION

1. Soak almonds in warm water to blanch. Remove the skin. Reserve a few for garnish and make a paste of the rest.

2. Slice almonds reserved for garnish and pistachio nuts. Wash and strain chironji.

3. Bring milk to a boil, simmer over low flame till milk coats the back of the spoon. Stir continuously.

4. Stir in almond paste dissolved in half a cup of water or milk and mix well. Add sugar and saffron and cook till sugar gets fully dissolved.

5. Chill and serve garnished with pista, chironji and almonds.

INGREDIENTS

Gram flour (*besan*) .... 4 cups

Cashewnuts 12-15

Almonds 12-15

Ghee .... 1 cup

Green cardamom powder ....1 tspn

Powdered sugar .... 2 cups

METHOD OF PREPARATION

1 Sieve the besan through a fine sieve and set aside.

2 Coarsely grind cashewnuts and almonds and keep aside.

3 Melt ghee in a kadai. Add besan, cook over low heat till besan is well done and gives an aroma. This normally takes about fifteen to twenty minutes. Add cardamom powder, ground cashewnuts and almonds. Stir and take it off the heat.

4 Let it cool for a while. Finally add the powdered sugar and mix well. You may use your hands to mix this.

5 Shape it into walnut sized spherical shape laddoos and store in an airtight container.

Chef's Tip: While serving Besan laddoos that have been kept for a few days in the refrigerator, warm them for fifteen to twenty seconds in the microwave. They will not only become soft but also seem freshly made.

BESAN KE LADDOO

INGREDIENTS

Mawa *(khoya)* ....1 ½ cups

Chenna .... ¼ cup

Cooking soda .... ¼ tspn

Flour *(maida)* ....3 tblspns

Cardamom powder ....¼ tspn

Ghee/oil ....to deep fry

Sugar ....2 cups

METHOD OF PREPARATION

1 Grate khoya and mash chenna. Keep aside.

2 Mix the two along with cooking soda, flour, cardamom powder and a little water to make into a soft dough.

3 Divide into sixteen equal portions and shape into balls.

4 Prepare a sugar syrup with equal quantity of water. Clear the syrup by removing the scum, if any.

5 Heat ghee/oil in a kadai. Add the balls and deep fry on low flame till golden in colour.

6 Drain and soak in the sugar syrup for atleast fifteen to twenty minutes before serving.

Chef's Tip : Temperature of the oil should be low or the jamuns will remain un-cooked from inside. You may stuff Gulab jamuns with saffron and pistachio nuts or mishri.

GULAB JAMUN

Malar ki kheer, Gulab jamun, Rasmalai

Jalebi, Chocolate burfi, Besan ke laddoo

JALEBI

INGREDIENTS

Flour (*maida*) ....1 ½ cups	Cardamom powder .... ½ tspn
Soda bi-carbonate (baking soda)....1 tspn	Ghee .... to deep fry
Sugar ....2 ½ cups	Yellow or saffron colour (optional) ....a pinch

METHOD OF PREPARATION

1 Mix flour and cooking soda. Add some water and make a smooth batter. Make sure that there are no lumps. Leave it overnight to ferment.

2 Mix it again, add a little water if required and make it into a pouring consistency.

3 Prepare sugar syrup by adding equal quantity of sugar and water. Add cardamom powder and cook it for twenty minutes.

4 Heat ghee in a jalebi tawi or a flat kadai or a frying pan. Pour batter into a jalebi cloth and then pour it into medium hot ghee giving it a jalebi shape. Start from outside to inside for better results.

5 Cook it from both sides till crisp. Remove and keep it in sugar syrup for at least five minutes before serving.

Chef's Tip : For the jalebi cloth, take some cloth and make a three mm hole in the centre. Jalebi making takes some practice and patience. To start with, try making individual jalebis and when you have perfected that, try making them together in a row.
To make crisp jalebis add a little rice flour to maida.

INGREDIENTS

Mawa *(khoya)* .... 2 cups	Cocoa powder .... 3 tblspns
Oil .... 2 tspns	Sugar .... $^1/_3$ cup

METHOD OF PREPARATION

1 Crumble mawa into fine granules. Grease a tray with oil and keep aside.

2 Cook mawa in a thick-bottomed pan, stirring continuously till it is completely melted and has a thick sauce like consistency. Do not colour.

3 Stir in sugar till it is completely dissolved and mawa is cooked.

4 Remove half of this mixture and pour onto the greased tray. For spreading the mawa evenly on the tray, hold it from two sides and rap it on a hard surface two or three times. Let it cool.

5 Keep the remaining half on a slow flame. Add the cocoa powder and mix well.

6 Pour the cocoa mixture over the earlier mixture. Let it cool completely. Cut into pieces and serve coated with silver leaves *(chandi ka vark)*, if desired.

Chef's Tip: Use an aluminium or steel tray for setting the Chocolate burfi as, while cutting, the knife may leave scratches on the surface of the plate used.

CHOCOLATE BURFI

MALPUA

INGREDIENTS

Milk .... 1 ½ lits
Mawa *(khoya)* .... 50 gms
Green cardamom 3
Flour *(maida)* ....3 tblspns
Ghee ....for deep frying
For the Sugar syrup
Water .... 2 cups

Natural yellow colour (optional) ...... ¼ tspn
Sugar ....2 cups
For Garnishing
Pistachio, chopped 15-20
Saffron .... a few strands

METHOD OF PREPARATION

1. Boil milk in a thick heavy-bottomed pan, reduce heat and simmer till it is reduced and reaches a coating consistency. Add grated khoya, and mix well. Bring it to room temperature.

2. Reserve two tblspns of sugar and form a one string sugar syrup with the rest of the sugar.

3. Add saffron to the sugar syrup.

4. Add flour and the reserved sugar to the reduced milk. Mix well and make a batter of pouring consistency using a little milk if required.

5. Heat ghee in a wide mouthed flat bottomed kadai. Pour a ladle full of batter to form a small pancake. Cook on slow to medium heat.

6. Turn it over when it starts to colour slightly. When both sides are done, drain and immerse in the sugar syrup.

7. Sprinkle a little of the chopped pistachio and saffron. Serve hot.

Chef's Tip : Serve hot Malpuas with chilled rabdi, it tastes divine.

INGREDIENTS

Shelled green peas ....1 cup	Green cardamom powder ....1 tspn	
Ghee ....½ cup	Pistachio nuts 20-25	
Milk ....1 ¼ litres	Raisins 20-25	
Sugar ....1 cup		

METHOD OF PREPARATION

1 Boil green peas for five minutes. Refresh in cold water and grind to a fine paste.

2 Heat ghee in a thick-bottomed pan, add green peas paste and cook for a few minutes, stirring constantly. Keep aside.

3 Boil milk and add it to the cooked green peas paste. Bring it to a boil. Cook on a slow flame for fifteen to twenty minutes or till the milk is reduced to half.

4 Add sugar, green cardamom powder, raisins and sliced pistachio nuts. Cook for about eight to ten minutes on a slow flame, stirring continuously. Serve chilled.

Chef's Tip : When you serve Matar ki kheer, initially serve it as Pista kheer, as most people are not very receptive to the idea of eating kheer made out of green peas. However disclose it later to prompt people to try a second helping.

MATAR KI KHEER

MOHAN THAL

INGREDIENTS

Gram flour *(besan)* ....2 cups	Sugar ....1 cup
Almonds 8-10	Cardamom powder ....¼ tspn
Pistachio nuts 8-10	Nutmeg *(jaiphal)* powder ....¼ tspn
Ghee ....2 tblspns + ½ cup	Milk ....4 tblspns

METHOD OF PREPARATION

1 Sieve the besan and discard the residue.

2 Slice almonds and pistachio nuts and set aside.

3 Heat two tblspns of ghee and four tblspns of milk. Pour this over the besan.

4 Mix thoroughly with your fingers so that no lumps are formed and it resembles bread crumbs. Pass it through a sieve again and set aside.

5 Make a sugar syrup with one cup sugar and three-fourth cup of water. Stir the sugar and water and then heat. The syrup should be a little more than one string consistency. Once ready, keep it aside.

6 Grease a thali and keep aside.

7 Heat half cup ghee in a kadai. Add the treated besan and cook on a low flame till it gives out an aroma and besan turns golden brown. Stir constantly.

8 Add cardamom powder and nutmeg powder. Remove from the flame and add the hot sugar syrup when the besan mixture is still hot. Mix continuously to ensure that no lumps are formed. Continue to mix till it reaches setting consistency.

9 Pour onto the greased thali and rap it on a flat surface to flatten it. Garnish with sliced almonds and pistachio nuts. Let it cool and set.

10 Cut into the required shape and serve.

INGREDIENTS

Split green gram, skinless
(*moong dal, dhuli*) .... 1 cup

Sugar .... 1 cup

Saffron .... a generous pinch

Milk .... ½ cup

Mawa *(khoya)* .... ¾ cup

Ghee .... 1 cup

Almonds 10-12

METHOD OF PREPARATION

1 Wash and soak the moong dal for six hours. Grind coarsely using very little water.

2 Prepare one string sugar syrup with the sugar and one and half cups of water.

3 Soak saffron in hot milk. Crumble mawa into fine granules. Blanch almonds in boiling hot water for five minutes. Cool and peel them, cut them into thin slivers.

4 Heat ghee in a thick-bottomed pan and add the ground moong dal. Keep stirring over a low flame till the dal turns golden brown. This needs time and patience. Do not rush through this step.

5 Add the sugar syrup and saffron milk, stir till they are thoroughly incorporated and the halwa is of dropping consistency. Add mawa and cook till it dissolves.

6 Serve hot, garnished with sliced almonds.

Chef's Tip: Add one tblspn besan to melted ghee before putting the ground moong dal. It helps in even cooking of ground moong dal and also avoids lump formation during cooking.

MOONG DAL
HALWA

PHIRNI

INGREDIENTS

Rice ....5 tblspns	Pistachio nuts 10-15
Saffron ....a generous pinch	Sugar ....¾ cup
Milk .... 1 lt	Green cardamom powder ....½ tspn

METHOD OF PREPARATION

1. Pick, wash and soak rice for half an hour and then grind it to a coarse paste.
2. Blanch pistachio nuts in hot water, cool, remove skin and slice.
3. Bring milk to a boil. Add rice paste dissolved in a little water or cold milk. Cook till rice is completely cooked. Stir constantly. Add saffron and mix well.
4. Add sugar, cardamom powder and cook till sugar is completely dissolved.
5. Pour into earthenware or china bowls and garnish with sliced pista.
6. Chill in a refrigerator for an hour before serving.

Chef's Tip : It is a good idea to grind green cardamom with a little sugar as otherwise the quantity of green cardamom may be too little to grind. You can store this in an airtight jar for use in sweet dishes and desserts.

INGREDIENTS

Chenna .... 250 gms   Sugar .... 4 cups
Pistachio nuts 10-12   Milk .... 2 lts
Refined flour (*maida*) .... 4 tblspns

METHOD OF PREPARATION

1 Crumble the chenna and mash it. Add two tblspns maida and mash again with the palm of your hand to make a dough.

2 Divide into sixteen equal portions, roll into balls and press slightly to flatten them.

3 Blanch pistachio nuts in hot water, cool, remove skin and slice.

4 Dissolve two cups of sugar in the same quantity of water, bring to a boil, add the rest of the flour dissolved in a little water.

5 Slowly lower the chenna balls in the boiling syrup and cook over high flame for ten minutes. Add half a cup of water and bring to a boil again. Cook for three minutes.

6 Meanwhile prepare a thin sugar syrup with one cup sugar and two cups of water.

7 Soak the cooked chenna balls in this syrup.

8 Boil the milk in a thick-bottomed pan, lower the flame and continue to boil till it is reduced to a thick consistency. Stir continuously.

9 Add the rest of the sugar to reduced milk and keep boiling till the sugar is dissolved. Take it off the fire, cool and refrigerate for an hour.

10 Squeeze the chenna balls and put them into the chilled and sweetened reduced milk. Refrigerate it for another half an hour.

11 Serve chilled, garnished with sliced pistachio.

Chef's Tip : Use chenna made from cow's milk. Best chenna is made by curdling cow's milk with leftover whey of chenna made earlier. The trick lies in curdling and the acid content should be just right, if it is too much, the chenna would become tough.

RASMALAI

GLOSSARY

English	Hindi	
Ingredients		
Almond	Badam	Used as a garnish for sweets and as an ingredient in pulaos and curries.
Asafoetida	Hing	A powerful seasoning, used to flavour curries.
Bay leaves	Tej patta	These dried leaves are used to flavour curries and rice.
Black cardamom	Badi ilaichi	Used for flavouring curries and pulaos.
Black gram	Urad (whole)	The split form, urad dal and whole urad is used to make curries.
Black peppercorn	Kali mirch	This hot, pungent spice is an important ingredient in hot garam masala. The pepper powder is often used in curries, rice and savoury dishes.
Capsicum	Simla mirch	Used as a vegetable and also in salads.
Caraway	Shah jeera	Used for flavouring curries and pulaos.
Carom seeds	Ajwain	Also known as Bishop's weed. Used as a part of batters, masalas and in savoury dishes.
Cashewnuts	Kaju	Used in sweets and pulao as a garnish and cashew paste is used to flavour and thicken curries.
Chick peas	Kabuli Chana, chole	Split chick peas - chana dal is used to make curries.
Chilli	Mirch	Green or dried red chillies or red chilli powder are used extensively in Indian cooking to make the food hot.
Cinnamon	Dalchini	These dry sticks are used to flavour curries and rice and is an ingredient in garam masala.
Clove	Laung	Used in both sweet and savoury dishes.
Coconut	Narial	An important part of South Indian cooking. The milk and flesh extracted from the coconut is used as a base for curries, soups, chutneys and sweets.
Coriander seeds	Dhania	Used whole and in the powdered form in curries and vegetables and as a part of garam masala.

Cottage cheese (Indian)	Paneer	Used in vegetables as well as a base in sweet dishes.
Cumin seeds	Jeera	Used whole or ground, it imparts a spicy, aromatic flavour to curries, pulaos and raitas. Light roasting in a dry pan enhances the aroma.
Curry leaves	Kadhi patta	Used fresh or dried, they have a warm, appetizing aroma and give a delicate, spicy flavour to the dish. Used extensively in South Indian cooking.
Dry mango powder	Amchur	Used in curries and vegetables to give sour and tangy taste.
Fennel	Saunf	These dried seeds used extensively to flavour curries and pickles, have a sweet aromatic flavour.
Fenugreek leaves	Methi	Fresh leaves are used as a vegetable and in paranthas. Dried leaves known as kasoori methi are used for seasoning curries.
Fenugreek seeds	Methi dana	Whole seeds are used for seasoning, whereas the powder is an essential ingredient of pickles. For best results, lightly roast.
Fresh cream	Malai	Used in sweets and some curries. Home-made malai can be obtained by letting boiled milk cool and skimming off the layer of fat that forms on the surface.
Garlic	Lehsoon	Often used whole or as paste, in combination with ginger to flavour curries and pulaos.
Ginger	Adrak	Used as fresh or in the paste form in curries and vegetables. Dried ginger root is sometimes used to flavour pickles.
Ginger powder	Saunth	This can be used in place of fresh ginger. Popular in Kashmiri food.
Gramflour	Besan	Ground gram/chana dal, used in many sweet and savoury dishes.
Green cardamom	Chhoti ilaichi	Used whole, as a part of garam masala and in the powdered form to flavour sweets and some rice dishes.

Green coriander	Hara dhania	Used in curries and vegetables as well as for garnishing.
Green gram	Moong	Used as whole, bean sprouts or split -- as dal. Skinless split gram (moong, dhuli) is used for making curries and halwa.
Green peas	Matar	These can be used fresh or frozen.
Honey	Shahad	Used as a sugar substitute.
Jaggery	Gud	A sugar substitute, imparts a delicate earthy taste to the dish.
Mace	Javantri/javitri	It is the outer covering of nutmeg. It has a delicate flavour and is used as an ingredient in masalas.
Mint	Pudina	These leaves are widely used in chutneys and as a flavouring for yogurt and in appetizers. Dried leaves are ground to make mint powder.
Mustard seeds	Rai/sarson	Whole seeds are used for tempering and as powder, in pickles.
Nutmeg	Jaiphal	The sweet-woody scent gives a special flavour to sweet dishes.
Okra (Lady's fingers)	Bhindi	Used as a vegetable.
Onion	Piaz	Chopped and as paste, it is used as a base in many curries and vegetables. Different gravies require different onion pastes. For instance, white gravies require boiled onion paste while red gravies use brown onion paste.
Onion seeds	Kalonji	Dry onion seeds are used in pickles and as a topping for Naans.
Pigeon peas	Toor	These in their split form are used to make curries.
Poppy seeds	Khus khus	Used to thicken curries.
Refined flour	Maida	Used as a base to make different Indian breads and also to make snacks.

Rose water	Gulab jal	Rose water and rose essence are especially used in Indian sweets like Gulab jamoons and in sherbets.
Saffron	Kesar	This rare and expensive spice is used in minute quantities to flavour milk-based sweets and sometimes in special curries and biryanis. To get maximum flavour, saffron should be dissolved in warm milk for about twenty minutes before use.
Semolina	Rawa	Used to make Indian breads like paranthas, puris and as a base in some sweets.
Sesame seeds	Til	The seeds are used in some sweets. Sesame paste is sometimes added to flavour and thicken the spicy curries. Sesame oil is used for cooking in some parts of the country. For better flavour, slightly roast the seeds until they jump.
Soda bi-carbonate	Baking soda	Used for raising the flour.
Star anise	Badiyan/Phoolchakri	This dried, reddish-brown fruit, used in small quantities, gives a distinctive aroma to the dish.
Sweet potato	Rataloo (Shakarkand)	This has a sweetish taste and can be fried, boiled, roasted or cooked in a gravy.
Tamarind	Imli	Added to curries to give a mild refreshing sour taste. Tamarind pulp, which can be stored in the refrigerator, is used more often in curries and chutneys. When combined with sugar and other spices, mixed with cold water, it makes a delightful cooling drink.
Turmeric	Haldi	The yellow-coloured powder of the turmeric root gives a distinct flavour and colour to the curries, vegetables and pulaos. It also has medicinal properties.
Wheat flour	Atta	Whole meal flour is used as a base to make different Indian breads.
Yogurt/Curd	Dahi	Yogurt is added to cooked dishes and also as a base for raitas, snacks like Dahi vadas and consumed in its liquid form as lassi or buttermilk.

Some Indian terms

Charoli seeds	Also known as Chironji. Used as garnish in sweets.
Chenna	A form of cottage cheese, used as a base for sweets like Rasagoola or rasmalai.
Garam masala	Spice powder. Lightly roast and grind the following ingredients to make the masala: Black cardamom 8-10; Green cardamom 15-20; Cinnamon 15-20 pieces (1" each); Cloves 1 tblspn; Mace 1 flower; Nutmeg 1; Peppercorn 1 tblspn; Cumin seeds 1/2 cup; Coriander seeds 2 tblspns.
Ghee	Clarified butter. Used as a cooking medium in some dishes instead of oil.
Goda masala	A spice powder, also called 'sweet mix', containing most of the ingredients from the garam masala, with extra Cumin seeds and whole dried red chillies.
Kokum	This sour, dry red fruit, also known as amsool or red mango is used in some curries for its sour flavour.
Masala	Spice powders. Indian cooking uses different kinds of masalas such as Garam masala, goda masala, chaat masala.
Mawa	Khoya. Used as a base for sweets and as a thickener in some curries.

Some Indian utensils

Degchi	A wide, thick-bottomed vessel.
Handi	A heavy-bottomed vessel, used to cook vegetables, curries, rice.
Kadai	A deep pan, mainly used for deep-frying.

Katori	A small bowl.
Patila	A large bowl, a thin-bottomed vessel.
Tandoor	A traditional clay oven fired by charcoal. Used for baking breads like Naan and Tandoori roti and for roasting meat, vegetables and paneer. The charcoal fire gives a smoked flavour to the dish.
Tawa	A thick, flat pan, used to make Indian breads like rotis, paranthas.
Tawi	A shallow frying pan, used for jalebis.
Thali	A metal plate.

Some cooking methods

Baste	Moisten with gravy or melted fat/butter during cooking.
Blanch	Immerse briefly in boiling water.
Broil	Roast/Lightly fry. Also a term used for cooking meat.
Deep frying	Fry in a lot of oil/ghee
Marinate	Soak meat, fish etc., before cooking, in a mixture of oil, spices, and for a few recipes, yogurt.
Puree	Make a soft pulp of vegetables or fruit and reduce to a smooth paste.
Roast	Heat/lightly fry, before grinding in cases of spices. Cook in an oven.
Sauté	Quickly fry in a little hot oil.
Temper	(Tadka, baghar) The first step in certain recipes: Heat oil. Add mustard seeds/cumin seeds to it. After they crackle, add the other spices/curry leaves.